Dedication

Lovingly dedicated to Matthew Craig McLeod,
our first-born son.
You are beloved, Matt, and your dad and I are well-pleased
with the life you are living.
Keep pursuing the Father, who does all things well!
You will never know how dearly you are loved,
how passionately you are prayed for,
and how fiercely you are believed in.
You are always, always in my heart.

CAROL MCLEOD

INVITING CHRIST INTO
EVERY ROOM

AT HOME IN YOUR *Heart*

WHITAKER
HOUSE

At Home in Your Heart
Inviting Christ into Every Room

Carol McLeod Ministries
P.O. Box 1294
Orchard Park, NY 14127
855-569-5433
www.carolmcleodministries.com

ISBN: 978-1-64123-803-8
eBook ISBN: 978-1-64123-804-5
Printed in the United States of America

Whitaker House
1030 Hunt Valley Circle
New Kensington, PA 15068
www.whitakerhouse.com

Library of Congress Cataloging-in-Publication Data (Pending)

1 2 3 4 5 6 7 8 9 10 11 ᴧᴧ 30 29 28 27 26 25 24 23 22

Contents

Part Eight: The Dining Room –
Serve a Generous Portion of Your Faith to Others

Part Nine: Knickknacks – Daily Wisdom for Your Heart

Introduction: Welcome Home!

*By wisdom a house is built, and by understanding it
is established; and by knowledge the rooms are filled with
all precious and pleasant riches.*
—Proverbs 24:3–4

You might suppose that your home is 83 East Academy Street...or 6555 Alleghany Road...or 16 Willow Lane. But it's not. You can frantically inspect every printed map and strategically pore over every listing in an address book, but you will never discover your actual home at a zip code, on a street, or in a city.

You may presume that your particular home consists of three bedrooms and a bathroom...or a massive family room...or a farmhouse kitchen. But again, your actual home has nothing to do with the floor plan that lies under the roof of the home in which you live.

Perhaps when you think of home, you remember the childhood house in which you hung stockings along the mantle on Christmas Eve, blew out candles on eighteen birthday cakes, and colored Easter eggs every spring! But even that home, where you began your journey and where you were shaped as an individual, is not your true home either. The home of your earliest memories will never be the home of your adult realities.

Your real home—this side of heaven, of course—is your heart. Your heart is where you live day in and day out. Your heart is the hidden but obvious home in which you live.

Your heart is where you collect clutter, but it is also where you receive company, fill up trash cans, and then remodel. The wonderful, miraculous part of you that is *vibrantly alive* lives within the canyons of your heart.

Your heart is home to your soul, which is the birthplace of your emotions. It is also where your thought life is framed. Many people are deceived into believing that their thought life begins in their minds, but this is not the case. Your thoughts and attitudes make themselves at home in your heart.

What about your habits? Where do *they* live? It is easy to discern that both good habits and bad habits, which efficiently determine the exact floor plan of your life, can easily be found residing in your heart. Even your dreams, which are often beyond your wildest imagination, can be found hanging out unassumingly in your heart.

Your heart is the part of you that sometimes longs to escape from its earthly address. Your heart feels constrained by the white picket fence that you so lovingly built around the parameters of your life. Your heart is the part of you that is never content with who you are or what you are becoming.

Your heart is your *real* home. It is the place where the "you" that *vitally* matters lives and breathes. This "you," who no one else knows, lives life with reckless abandon, glorious intensity, and holy intention in your heart.

Your heart is the most sacred part of your life because it is there that Christ has lovingly taken up residence. If you have invited Him in, He lives in your heart, and you should honor His presence day after day after day.

But perhaps an important question for you and me to answer is, *"What else is living in my heart with Christ?"*

Have you allowed attitudes, habits, and dreams that should not be a part of your life to live side by side with Christ? Maybe some of our hearts need a deep and detailed housecleaning due to the clutter that has accumulated, the trash that has yet to be taken out, and the out-of-date décor that we foolishly insist doesn't look all that bad!

Jesus will live in your heart no matter what condition it is in. However, once Jesus takes residence in one's heart and shares that personal address, He wants to clean until His hands bleed.

Jesus wants to paint your heart the color of freshly fallen snow.

Jesus longs to redecorate the house that you call home into a sanctuary of hope and peace.

He will gently move around priorities, set out the trash, and replace every outdated attitude with His unconditional love and inexpressible joy.

Jesus can take a dilapidated shack that has been built with rotten wood and miraculously turn it into a glorious temple! He can transform an unstable and cracked foundation into one that is steady and secure. He can take a home that has been literally demolished by the storms of life and rebuild it into a palace fit only for a King.

My friend, not only will He be more at home in your sparkling, restored, and renewed heart, but the greatest miracle of all is that so will you! You will love what He does with your heart and you will gulp in the splendid atmosphere that only His dear presence provides. His goal, as the Divine Builder, is to fashion your heart into His home.

As you walk through the front door of your heart, holding His hand, you will find the place where you were always meant to belong and the place that wondrously calls your name. At last—you are home with Him!

You will find contentment in the heart that you call home when He holds the keys. As you examine the masterpiece that He has created, you will be amazed by the wonder and wisdom that His lordship has brought. Most of all, you will find that His presence has filled your home with joy!

I'd love to invite you to come with me on this restorative journey that will transform your heart into a home of comfort, stability, and peace. We will discover nooks and crannies in your heart that have been wonderfully designed for learning and growing. We will dispose of every outdated appliance and replace each one with eternal truth; we will repurpose every dream into a masterpiece of prayer. As we allow the Lord to be the Architect, the Builder, and our sure Foundation, our hearts will become a place of divine residence. And we will each utter with a whisper of worship, "Welcome home, Jesus. Welcome home!"

> Imagine yourself as a living house.
> God comes in to rebuild that house....
> You thought you were going to be made
> into a decent little cottage:
> but He is building a palace.
> He intends to come and live in it Himself.
> —C. S. Lewis, *Mere Christianity*

PART ONE:
THE FOUNDATION

He will be the sure foundation for your times,
a rich store of salvation and wisdom and knowledge;
the fear of the LORD is the key to this treasure.
—Isaiah 33:6 (NIV)

Over the next seven days, we will be taking a long, intense look at the foundational issues of life. Through Scripture, we will examine how to build a strong foundation in our hearts that will ensure our lives will become all that they were meant to be.

Foundational Issues

Shortly after their wedding, a young couple wished to buy a home in which they would start a family, create precious memories, and build a life of pure happiness. What these sweet newlyweds lacked in money, they more than compensated for in a boundless and enthusiastic amount of energy. This naive yet earnest couple knew that a "fixer-upper" was all they were able to afford. They also realized that their difficult home search might require a top-notch realtor who was familiar with every home on the market. After diligent research and endless questioning of friends and family members, they found the top realtor in town and went on a ferocious hunt for their own dream home.

Day after day after day, they met the prosperous realtor and looked at every run-down, vacant house in town. This dynamic and relentless duo inspected the windows, the size of the rooms, the cabinetry, and the condition of the bathrooms. Very sure of their priorities, they were intent on not compromising even the smallest detail.

The realtor, who was a force to be reckoned with, looked the total picture of success; she was stylishly dressed in a designer suit with coordinating shoes while brandishing a pricey handbag.

After the couple had enthusiastically perused each home, she would quietly take off her gloves, lay her hat and purse on the dilapidated front porch, and crawl under the house. Then, without fanfare, she would crawl out again, wipe the dirt from her expensive suit, and simply declare, "No, I won't let you buy this house."

The disappointed young couple stood forlornly on the steps of the vacant yet potential-filled home while the realtor marched off to her fancy car.

Finally, after weeks of house hunting, the young couple and the realtor came upon a true monstrosity, a century-old home that had been uninhabited for nearly half of those years. The couple stood outside gasping for breath while trying to think of a tactful way to fire the realtor; they were convinced she had lost her very successful mind. The realtor quietly climbed under the home, as was her custom. This time, as she crawled out from under the rodent-laden home, she said with great joy, "This is it! This is the home for you!"

The realtor knew a secret that the young couple had not possessed the wisdom to consider: it's all about the foundation. The realtor knew that even a lovely home without a solid foundation would never stand the test of time. A weak and wavering foundation would be the demise of the home and therefore the demise of the newlyweds' dreams.

As you inspect the qualities that you desire in a life of honor, security, and hope, have you taken a long look at the foundation upon which you have built your life? It is vital to remember that *your foundation determines what you have the capacity to become.*

Heart Inspection

What is the single most important part of your life?

What are some of the attitudes and habits that might compromise the foundation of your life?

List some words that describe the type of life that you would like to build:

Heartfelt Prayer

Lord Jesus, I just want You. I want what You want for my life more than what I want for my life. I ask that You would help me to trust You and to obey You every day. In Jesus's name, I pray. Amen.

Eternal Words

> *For no one is empowered to lay an alternative foundation other than the good foundation that exists, which is Jesus Christ!*
>
> —1 Corinthians 3:11 TPT

Digging Even Deeper

Read 1 Corinthians 3.

DAY 2
Is Anyone Home?

Is anybody home? Is anyone truly at home in your heart?

Your heart was intended to be the dwelling place of someone other than you! Imagine that! If all that you have filled your heart with are *your* opinions, *your* desires, *your* emotions, and *your* frustrations, your one-of-a-kind heart will quickly become an overcrowded hiding place of personal pain and of unmet destiny.

Who is at home in your heart? Whose presence have you invited into the living space there?

There is nothing sadder than an abandoned home; often the roof commences to sag, the porch begins to collapse, and the windows are cracked and broken. Four solid walls and a stellar roof will never be all that it takes to create a loving home. A home requires occupancy. A shell of a home that is devoid of kindred friendship and loving family will soon lose its purpose and its vitality.

A home was always meant to be a structure that is gloriously lived in! A house is not a home until it is filled with contagious laughter, unselfish love, and the consummate joy that accompanies lasting companionship.

However, if the occupants of the home are only temporary guests, the joy will not last long. And if the occupants are unruly, disruptive, and selfish, peace and kindness will quickly run away from home!

Who lives in the home of your heart? Who have you invited into the heart that is uniquely and sumptuously yours and yours alone?

Today is a day of consideration and inspection. Would you inspect who and what lives in your heart? Would you ask yourself the probing question, "Who lives in my heart?"

The stunning and eternal truth is that there is only one Occupant who truly matters. There is only one Guest who should be invited to stay long-term. There is only one Friend whose presence turns a heart into a home. There is only One. Have you invited Him in?

He should never be considered a mere guest, for His presence will determine the very strength of your life. Jesus should always be first and foremost; He should be the sure Cornerstone upon which all other building materials, both eternal and temporary, are laid.

What deep joy is experienced when the foundation of your life is Christ and Christ alone! What unmatched hope will reside in the corners of your heart when everything else bows to King Jesus! What comfort will be yours when you determine that nothing else matters but Him!

Heart Inspection

Can you identify the emotions or attitudes that have made your heart their home?

Have you invited Jesus into your heart? A simple yes or no will do.

Heartfelt Prayer

Lord Jesus, everything I am is Yours. Everything I have is Yours. I invite You to come into my heart and to forgive me of my sins. I am a sinner, and You are a Savior, so we are a perfect match! Thank You for Your eternal presence in the deepest places of my heart. In Jesus's name, I pray. Amen.

Eternal Words

Lord, you have always been our eternal home, our hiding place from generation to generation. —Psalm 90:1 TPT

Digging Even Deeper

Read Psalm 90.

Location! Location! Location!

Jesus had just reached the peak of the greatest sermon He had ever preached. It was a Mount Everest moment in the lives of the people who were listening to the voice of Christ as He taught about eternity past and eternity yet to come.

Perhaps Jesus paused before speaking these last few words to the people gathered where the air was thin but the view was breathtaking. As the crowd eagerly anticipated the pregnant words of the One whom they lovingly called "Teacher," Jesus brought the most remarkable sermon of all time to a stirring conclusion.

> *Now why do you call Me, "Lord, Lord," and do not do what I say? Everyone who comes to Me and hears My words and acts on them, I will show you whom he is like: he is like a man building a house, who dug deep and laid a foundation on the rock; and when there was a flood, the river burst against that house and yet it could not shake it, because it had been well built. But the one who has heard and has not acted accordingly is like a man who built a house on the ground without a foundation; and the river burst against it and it immediately collapsed, and the ruin of that house was great.* —Luke 6:46–49

Jesus was an expert both in wisdom and Scriptures. He had been taught the Scriptures since He was a young boy running through the dusty streets of Nazareth. Surely He knew very well the proverb that taught, *"When the whirlwind passes, the wicked is no more, but the righteous has an everlasting foundation"* (Proverbs 10:25).

Jesus was also an expert in life. A carpenter and the son of a carpenter, Jesus had probably built many homes by the time He was thirty years old. When He spoke of foundations, He knew their importance in a practical sense. He wasn't merely spouting intangible word pictures, but He was teaching from His very own life experience.

I wonder if Jesus had some dealings with a foolish person who demanded that his brand-new dream home be constructed on sand. Palestine had many gullies that were pleasant, shaded little hollows in the summertime—and filled with rushing torrents of vicious water in the winter months. If a builder were shortsighted, he would lay the foundation in the riverbed and think it suitable. In winter, this masterpiece of first-century architecture would disintegrate like sugar in water. This house would be here today...and gone tomorrow.

The wise man, conversely, searched for sustainable and immovable rock. The long-sighted builder traveled far and wide, looking for a strong, stable, never-changing place on which to lay the foundation. It was decidedly more difficult than building on the sand and made the process excruciatingly longer; an experienced builder knew that building on the rock took more labor and was more expensive than building on the sand. There was not even a question if this home would withstand the torrential downpours of Palestine because its foundation was on the rock!

Where have you laid the foundation of your life? Have you built your foundation in the sand? Does your foundation perhaps lie smack in the middle of the river gully? Perhaps you have built your life on cultural expectations or, like many others, have built your life on recreation and entertainment.

The only sure foundation is Christ Jesus. Have you built your life upon Him?

Heart Inspection

What does it mean to you personally to *build your life on the sand?*

_____

_____

What does it mean to you personally to *build your life on the rock?*

_____

_____

What is to be gained by building your life on the Rock of Jesus Christ?

_____

_____

Heartfelt Prayer

Lord Jesus, I come to You today knowing that I have often built my life on temporary pleasure rather than on the security and stability of all that You are. Today, Lord, I choose to begin again. I choose to build my life on Your hope, on the salvation that comes only from You and on Your Holy Spirit. In Jesus's name, I pray. Amen.

Eternal Words

Trust in the LORD forever, for in GOD the LORD, we have an everlasting Rock.   —Isaiah 26:4

Digging Even Deeper

Read Luke 6:17–49 and Isaiah 26:1–9.

The Inspection

Let's rejoin Jesus on the mountain again today as we inspect the foundation that we are attempting to build in our hearts. Lean in and listen again to His stirring sermon and continue to gather eternal truth that will help you build an unshakable foundation.

> *Now why do you call Me, "Lord, Lord," and do not do what I say? Everyone who comes to Me and hears My words and acts on them, I will show you whom he is like: he is like a man building a house, who dug deep and laid a foundation on the rock; and when there was a flood, the river burst against that house and yet it could not shake it, because it had been well built. But the one who has heard and has not acted accordingly is like a man who built a house on the ground without a foundation; and the river burst against it and it immediately collapsed, and the ruin of that house was great.* —Luke 6:46–49

Jesus said, *"Everyone who hears these words of Mine, and acts on them, will be like a wise man who built his house on the rock"* (Matthew 7:24). If a rock-solid foundation is the goal of your life, you must listen to the words of Jesus and not to the wiles of culture.

However, Jesus also said that *listening* to the Word of God was only the first step. He said you also have to *act* upon the Word of God if a sure foundation is the goal. *Listening* to the Word of God is merely where it begins because *doing* what the Word of God says is an equally important part of establishing your foundation in Christ.

Listening to the Word might be likened to choosing the right location on which to build the foundation of your life. But acting on the Word of God is taking the ax or the chisel and going after that spot on the Rock! If all you have is knowledge of the Word, you will become a know-it-all. However, if you have knowledge and then act on it, you become a teacher, a scholar, or even a world-changing Christian.

So, as Jesus told the crowd on the mountaintop, you must hear His Word and then act upon it. You must listen solely to Him and then you must do what He says.

But prove yourselves doers of the word, and not just hearers who deceive themselves.
                                                    —James 1:22

Listening to His Word, hiding it in your heart, and then acting upon it can be summed up in one word: *obedience!*

The primary action step that you must take in order to assure a firm foundation in your life is to obey Jesus. When the winds of life blow—and they will—you will not be shaken. And when the storms of life invade—and they will—you will still be standing strong!

He established the earth upon its foundations, so that it will not totter forever and ever.   —Psalm 104:5

When you do things God's way rather than your own way, you will never totter and the foundation of your one glorious life will stand firm and secure.

Heart Inspection

What is your favorite Scripture verse? Write it out here:

_____

_____

How has the Lord asked you to obey Him lately?

_____

_____

If you could do anything for the Lord, what would it be?

_____

_____

Heartfelt Prayer

Lord Jesus, inspect my heart today. My deepest desire is to obey You completely, fully, and instantly. I declare today, "Not my will, but Your will be done in me." In Jesus's wonderful name, I pray. Amen.

Eternal Words

> Nevertheless, the firm foundation of God stands, having this seal: "The Lord knows those who are His;" and, "Everyone who names the name of the Lord is to keep away from wickedness."
>
> —2 Timothy 2:19

Digging Even Deeper
Read James 1.

DAY 5

Strong Yet Beautiful

For we are God's fellow workers; you are God's field, God's building. According to the grace of God which was given to me, like a wise master builder I laid a foundation, and another is building on it. But each person must be careful how he builds on it. For no one can lay a foundation other than the one which is laid, which is Jesus Christ. Now if anyone builds on the foundation with gold, silver, precious stones, wood, hay, or straw, each one's work will become evident; for the day will show it because it is to be revealed with fire, and the fire itself will test the quality of each one's work.
—1 Corinthians 3:9–13

Isn't it amazing to know that we are not cookie-cutter Christians? Each of us is a rare individual and *one of a kind* in God's eyes. We are all unique! Deliciously so!

According to the Bible, God allows you to add some materials of your own choice upon your foundation. Personality, gifts, preferences, and individuality are highlighted as we choose the materials that will complete the foundation that has been laid.

Pure gold people are true from the inside out; they possess not a shred of guile or hypocrisy. Golden people are givers because they know that life is about others, not themselves. If you desire to add gold to your foundation, you will be a giver and not a taker! Golden people are filled with pure joy!

Silver people are faithful servants of God. They serve God no matter the cost or the season. Silver people are the best Sunday school teachers, the kindest mothers-in-law, and the very truest of friends. Silver people can simply be called *servants*.

Precious stones are those folks who use their talents for God. They find fulfillment in giving glory to the Lord and not to self. Precious stones are on the worship team, or they might be the intercessors of the church. Precious stones make the foundation stunningly attractive.

Wooden people, on the other hand, can be serviceable only if they are publicly appreciated. They are not the first to volunteer, but if asked, they just might come and help out once or twice a year. They don't attend church every Sunday, but if they are not too tired or if the weather is good, they will make an effort to be in the house of the Lord.

If you are adding straw to the foundation of your heart, you might be scratchy and smelly! You may be hurting other people's feelings with your words, your actions, and your attitudes.

If anyone's work which he has built on it remains, he will receive a reward. If anyone's work is burned up, he will suffer loss; but he himself will be saved, yet only so as through fire. Do you not know that you are a temple of God and that the Spirit of God dwells in you? If anyone destroys the temple of God, God will destroy that person; for the temple of God is holy, and that is what you are.

—1 Corinthians 3:14–17

Your heart is God's dwelling place. You are more precious to God than you could ever imagine! Your foundation should not only be beautiful, it should also be generous and serviceable. God uses us as His dwelling place! He deeply desires to live in our hearts in order to accomplish His plan in the world.

Are you beginning to understand the importance of the foundation of your heart? Your life is all about Him! Your heart is all about Him! Your foundation is all about Him!

Heart Inspection

As you read the list of foundational attributes, what type of material have you added to your foundation?

_____

_____

Think of a time when you went through a fire—a difficult time in life. How did this time reveal your true character?

_____

_____

Heartfelt Prayer

Lord Jesus, burn up the straw in my heart. I long to be a person of pure gold intent, unselfish service, and anointed creativity. Jesus, would You use me in Your kingdom in powerful and magnificent ways? In Jesus's name, I pray. Amen.

Eternal Words

They sang, praising and giving thanks to the LORD, saying, "For He is good, for His favor is upon Israel forever." And all the people shouted with a great shout of joy when they praised the LORD, because the foundation of the house of the LORD was laid. —Ezra 3:11

Digging Even Deeper

Read Ezra 3.

A Crack in the Foundation

A crack in the foundation of one's home is absolutely devastating! Cracks in an otherwise stable foundation are able to appear when the home is old or new; they are generally precipitated by a change in the ground conditions under the foundation. When one side of a home's foundation settles lower than the other, it causes uneven tension, and the cracking that then occurs is nothing short of calamitous. It is wildly expensive and ultimately time-consuming to repair a crack in the foundation of a home. There are times when the occupants must actually abandon the home and wait for the costly, arduous repairs to be made.

Is there a crack in the foundation of your heart? One is sure to appear when you choose fear over faith and worry instead of hope. Simply put, a crack in the foundation of your heart will always be birthed in a lack of trust.

But as for me, I trust in You, Lord, I say, "You are my God."
—Psalm 31:14

Life is a classroom, isn't it? Every day that is spent this side of heaven's glory is a decisive lesson in how to navigate pain and earthly disappointment, yet still keep one's foundation intact. When we default to doubt in the middle of circumstantial instability, it is then, in that tenuous moment, that the tension that predisposes cracks will certainly appear.

Storms in life will happen: that is a certainty. Obstacles in life will appear: that is a certainty. Mountains will stand in the way and refuse to move: that is a certainty. However, a crack in the foundation of your heart should never appear! The way to avoid a crack in the stability of your heart is to trust Jesus every day.

Because you know Jesus, who is the author and perfecter of your faith, you can trust and not be afraid! (See Hebrews 12:2.)

Because you are assured that all power has been given to Him, you can respond with wholehearted trust when life seems upside down! (See Matthew 28:18.)

Because you know that the God of David, Daniel, Moses, Ruth, and Esther is the God of you, you can sleep with peace and arise with joy! (See Psalm 102:24–28.)

Because you know that He is good and that He works all things together for good, you can smile at the future. (See Romans 8:28.)

For our heart rejoices in Him, because we trust in His holy name.
—Psalm 33:21

Trust is a foundational issue in the heart of a believer in Jesus Christ. If you choose to panic, the condition of your heart will give way to a crack. If you choose to wail with frustration and worry in the night hours, the crack will grow even bigger and become more visible. However, if you *"trust in the LORD with all your heart and do not lean on your own understanding"* (Proverbs 3:5), He will protect your heart with His power and with His peace.

Heart Inspection

What are you currently worried about?

_____

_____

Are you able to give your worry and disappointment to your good, good Father today?

_____

_____

What does the word "trust" mean to you?

_____

_____

Heartfelt Prayer

Lord Jesus, would You forgive me for choosing to worry about my future rather than trusting You with it? Would You give me the strength that I need today to put all my trust in You? I declare, Father God, that You are in control and that You are accomplishing what concerns me. In Jesus's name, I pray. Amen.

Eternal Words

Trust in the LORD and do good; live in the land and cultivate faithfulness. Delight yourself in the LORD; and He will give you the desires of your heart. Commit your way to the LORD, trust also in Him, and He will do it.   —Psalm 37:3–5

Digging Even Deeper
Read Psalm 31.

DAY 7

The Cornerstone

So then you are no longer strangers and foreigners, but you are fellow citizens with the saints, and are of God's household, having been built on the foundation of the apostles and prophets, Christ Jesus Himself being the cornerstone, in whom the whole building, being fitted together, is growing into a holy temple in the Lord, in whom you also are being built together into a dwelling of God in the Spirit.
—Ephesians 2:19–22

The cornerstone is the very first stone set in the foundation of a building; all other stones will be set in reference to this first, premiere stone. The cornerstone determines the position of the entire structure and is the most critical stone of a building. The Bible is calling you today to choose Jesus Christ as the cornerstone of your life.

You get to select what stone, or what priority, you deem of greatest consequence and therefore as the cornerstone of your heart. No one will force you to choose Christ as your cornerstone; it is your choice and your choice alone. Some people choose other priorities such as money, family, education, travel, or exercise as a cornerstone. However, those wobbling cornerstones will never offer stability or the abundant life that only Christ can give. All of those other things can fit into your life after you have chosen your cornerstone.

The cornerstone ensures that a building will be stable through shifting sands and through the storms that assail. Jesus is that Rock-solid stone in your life! No mountain can move you, no storm can destroy you, and no enemy can bully you! Jesus is your cornerstone!

You will never be all that you were meant to be without His stability, His sacrifice, and His wisdom. He is able to fill up in you all that is missing in your own humanity. And, miracle of all miracles, it is His vitality that causes you to grow into a sanctuary in which God chooses to dwell. He makes you more captivating than you could ever be without Him.

Did you know that when you choose Christ as your cornerstone, the amazing building blocks in your foundation are the great men and women of faith who came before you? Your very life has *"been built on the foundation of the apostles and prophets"* (Ephesians 2:19).

Ruth's faithfulness has been added to your foundation; Abraham's friendship with God has been melted into your very core. Esther's courage and boldness have given you a resolve that you would never have on your own and David's heart of worship sings within the deep places of your soul. Daniel's fierce mind, Noah's obedience, and Jonah's resilience are all a nonnegotiable part of your lineage in Jesus Christ.

God has chosen your heart to be His beautiful home. He is in love with you and you are in love with Him! Even in our weakness, His strength is glorified. Even in our pain, He heals us. Even in our foolishness, He gives us the wisdom of the ages.

I am more than I could ever be because of my cornerstone. How little have I understood how much the God of creation would so deeply desire to dwell within my little heart! The truth that is poignantly apparent is how deeply I need Him. My life would be war-torn without His peaceful presence. My heart would be ripped into shreds without His sweet comfort. I would stay in a continual state of melancholy without His promised joy.

When you choose Christ as your cornerstone, faith as your foundation, and the God of Abraham, Isaac, and Jacob as your sanctuary, your life will be a shining demonstration of the One whom you serve. Who wouldn't want a heart that was built upon Him?!

Heart Inspection

Who is your favorite Old Testament Bible character?

_____

_____

What attribute do you most admire in that person from biblical history?

_____

_____

What do you love the most about being a Christian?

_____

_____

Heartfelt Prayer

Jesus, I want to be just like You! I want Your strength, Your joy, and Your wisdom! Thank You for wanting to live in my heart. In Jesus's name, I pray. Amen.

Eternal Words

"See, I lay a stone in Zion, a chosen and precious cornerstone, and the one who trusts in him will never be put to shame." Now to you who believe, this stone is precious. But to those who do not believe, "The stone the builders rejected has become the cornerstone."

—1 Peter 2:6–7 NIV

Digging Even Deeper

Read Ephesians 2.

Part Two:
The Blueprints – The Word of God

Down through the years I turned to the Bible
and found in it all that I needed.
—Ruth Bell Graham

Now that the foundation of our heart is strong and solid, it's time
to look at other aspects of our hearts. As you decide how to live
a life that honors Christ, you must use the Word of God as your
inerrant truth. The Bible is your honored blueprint for living.

DAY 8
Let Me See the Blueprints!

Building a home is an arduous, painstaking, and strenuous process. If your goal is to build an uncommon life that will honor the commitment you have made to Christ, you will need to carefully examine the blueprints.

When a bricklayer wants to know where the cornerstone is to be laid, he cries out, "Blueprints! Let me see the blueprints!"

When the plumber needs to know where to place the intricate pipe system, he demands, "Blueprints! Let me see the blueprints!"

And when the expert carpenter arrives on the scene to oversee the framing of the home, his words are much the same: "Blueprints! Let me see the blueprints!"

The blueprints are the single determining factor in the durability, cost, and formation of the home. No decisions are made, no nails are hammered, and no windows or doors are established without the express direction of the blueprints.

My friend, you too have been given a blueprint in the building of your heart. God, the finest Master Builder in all of recorded history, has provided an eternal blueprint for your life. For thousands of years, the blueprint that you have been given has enabled men and women to build a life that is simply incomparable. This wonderful blueprint is known as the Bible.

If you deeply desire life at its finest, a shelter in the time of stormy weather, and a home that will be the treasure chest of lovely memories, you must use the blueprint that your Master Builder has provided for you. The building code established in the Word of God will guarantee that your heart will become the home of your dreams. However, you will never establish such a home without studying the blueprints.

You must not foolishly believe that you can cast a quick glance at the Word of God and instantly know what it takes to build an exceptional life. You must seriously, quietly, and daily study the Bible. Some people forlornly suppose that reading the Bible every day is a difficult task, but that is just not true. I hope that you will quickly realize that by daily dedicating your life to reading the Word, you are apt to experience rich joy and dynamic strength. You will discover with millions of others what a delight it is to dig for gold in the unmatched, powerful, restorative, and miraculous Word of God.

Now, it is your turn to exclaim, "Blueprints! Let me see the blueprints!"

Heart Inspection

Do you currently have a daily time set aside for the reading of the Word of God?

_____

_____

Why or why not?

_____

_____

What are some of the obstacles that keep you from reading the Word of God every day? Be honest!

_____

_____

Heartfelt Prayer

Jesus, I pray that You would speak to me through the Word of God each day as I read it. I pray that Your Holy Spirit would give to me revelation knowledge that I have never before known or acknowledged. Speak, Lord, because I am listening to You as I read the Bible. In Jesus's name, I pray. Amen.

Eternal Words

God has prescribed the right way to live: obeying his laws with all our hearts. How I long for my life to bring you glory as I follow each and every one of your holy precepts! Then I'll never be ashamed, for I take strength from all your commandments. I will give my thanks to you from a heart of love and truth. And every time I learn more of your righteous judgments, I will be faithful to all that your Word reveals—so don't ever give up on me! —Psalm 119:4–8 TPT

Reading the Blueprint

Read Psalm 119:1–24.

DAY 9
An Intuitive Question

If you have never seen one, you might be wondering, "Now...what exactly *are* the blueprints?" Let me assure you that you have just asked a very intuitive question that deserves a specific answer!

The blueprints are detailed drawings, containing specifications and documents that have been approved by the builder of the home. A blueprint features documentation that fully describes the quality of the materials needed to complete the building of a stable and trustworthy home. It includes the size of the rooms, which way the doors will swing open, the type of oven planned (gas or electric) and its location, as well as placement of sinks, toilets, and more—all of the details that go into building a home. The blueprint is used to obtain precise estimates for the total cost of the home; it also explains why excellent homes require so much money.

The Bible is our detailed description that contains the specifications of living an abundant life that has been fully approved by our Builder. The Bible also clearly and repeatedly informs believers in Jesus Christ of the quality of choices that are necessary in establishing His lordship in our hearts.

The Bible sets forth a lifestyle that is extremely costly to the person who has decided to give her whole heart to Christ and to His unshakable kingdom. You will be doling out large sums of commitment, discipline, time, and sacrifice in order to establish a home that is welcoming to Jesus. I can assure you, however, that your sacrifice will never match the sacrifice that He has made on your behalf!

As you design your life in accordance with the principles found only in the Word of God, you are allowing Him to establish Himself as the chief cornerstone. As you devour the Word of God on a daily basis, you are welcoming His dear presence into every corner and into every hidden spot of your heart.

If you ignore the blueprints that have been given to you in the establishment of your heart, you will be making a grave error in judgment indeed. When the culture shouts at you, the Word of God will whisper the truth of eternity in response. When sin calls your name, the Bible responds with a hushed but powerful assurance that God knows best.

When your emotions deceive you, the Word of God will complete you and sustain you with sweet comfort and unrelenting nourishment.

It is your choice, however. How much of the Word do you want? How much of the Word do you need to build a heart of eternal joy? Will you lay down your own preferences and desires and then pick up the blueprint of Christ? Will you?

Heart Inspection

What is the cost of building a life that is honoring to Christ? Be specific.

_____

_____

Is there any area in your life in which you have ignored the principles of Scripture?

_____

_____

What is a practical choice that you can make today in order to accept the guidance of the Word rather than ignore it?

_____

_____

Heartfelt Prayer

Jesus, I need You and I need the wisdom of Your Word. I pray that the Bible would go to all of the deep places in my heart. Father, rule and overrule in my heart with Your truth. In Jesus's name, I pray. Amen.

Eternal Words

How can a young man stay pure? Only by living in the Word of God and walking in its truth. I have longed for you with the passion of my heart; don't let me stray from your directions! I consider your Word to be my greatest treasure, and I treasure it in my heart to keep me from committing sin's treason against you. —Psalm 119:9–11 TPT

Reading the Blueprint

Read Psalm 119:25–48.

DAY 10

The Mystery Solved

I am a great observer of people—all types of people! However, I especially love to observe Christians who are grappling with difficult circumstances in life. As I closely examine these believers in Jesus Christ, my mind is filled with questions that deserve an answer!

Why are some Christians gloriously victorious while others seem to live in constant defeat? Why?

How do some Christians discover joy even in the midst of great sorrow while others never experience deep happiness although their lives are filled with blessings? Why?

What enables some Christians to find deep meaning and rich purpose while living simple lives in ordinary ways while others are caught in a continual maze of, "Who am I?!" "Why am I?" and "Where am I?"

After heartfelt prayer and continual observation, I have realized that the Christians who are living victoriously, joyfully, and purposefully are the ones who have solved the mystery! They have discovered the key that unlocks the door to abundant Christian living. This age-old mystery is solved when a person daily reads the Word of God. You are given the key to peace and hope when you open your Bible and enthusiastically drink it in!

The Bible is not a flat book like *Gone with the Wind* or *Little Women*; rather, it is a rich and energetic deposit of the thoughts and Words of God Himself! The Bible is living and active, able to do a wondrous miracle in your very heart.

For the word of God is living and active, and sharper than any two-edged sword, even penetrating as far as the division of soul and spirit, of both joints and marrow, and able to judge the thoughts and intentions of the heart. —Hebrews 4:12

We all have issues that only the Word of God can heal; we all have human pain that only the Bible can alleviate. As you open the Word, read the Word, devour the Word, and fall in love with the Word of God, you will become the woman you have always desired to be! The Bible is God's love letter to His bride and is filled with the wisdom of the ages.

Heart Inspection

What is your favorite Bible verse? Write it out below. Have you memorized it yet?

_____

_____

Make it your goal to read your Bible about five to ten minutes each day this week. Underline the verses that speak to you.

_____

_____

Heartfelt Prayer

Father, I pray today that the Word of God would pierce my soul and my heart. I pray that the Word of God would reveal my weakness and fill me with Your strength. In Jesus's name, I pray. Amen.

Eternal Words

I will bless the LORD who has advised me; indeed, my mind instructs me in the night. I have set the LORD continually before me; because He is at my right hand, I will not be shaken. —Psalm 16:7–8

Reading the Blueprint

Read Psalm 119:49–72.

Blessed by the Begats

When I attended a Christian university in the mid-1970s, one of my greatest gifts was a friend and future roommate named Debby. Debby had short, black curly hair; mine was long, straight, and blond. Debby was petite and a little fireball; I was of average size and an introvert. Debby was the consummate life of the party; I didn't even know what a party was! Debby has always kept me from being boring, and I have kept her out of trouble.

Debby's mom had died of cancer when Debby was only twelve years old; understandably, Debby's teenage years had been much different than mine had been. At her mother's funeral, the pastor's wife had taken Debby aside and kindly told her, "Debby, the only way you are going to make it through this great grief is by reading your Bible."

Debby received the wisdom that this compassionate woman had offered and devoured the Bible on a daily basis. When Debby and I were college roommates, she would arise every morning at 5:30 a.m., put on her thick glasses, and go into the hallway to read her Bible for half an hour.

As the years passed by, Debby and I stayed in touch with Christmas cards and our annual birthday phone calls. As we closed our often expensive but necessary phone conversations, I always was sure to ask, "Debby, are you still reading your Bible?"

"Yep! Every day," was her sincere response.

On April 30, 2005, Debby's husband Steve was killed in a tragic accident. I called Debby early the next morning to pray for her and encourage her, even though we lived a thousand miles from each other.

Intermixed with tears, thanksgiving, and emotion, I finally asked her, "Debby, did you read your Bible today?"

This was her response:

Yes, I did, Carol. I opened to my daily plan and read in First Chronicles chapters one through eight. As I read the verses, I got so mad at the Holy Spirit that I nearly closed my Bible! The place where I was supposed to read today was just eight looong chapters of people's names. It is filled with *begats* and names of people I could never pronounce and who I had never even heard of! These weren't the big names of the Bible—you know, like Daniel, David, and Moses. It was people like Arpachshad, Reuel, and Timna.

As I sat with my Bible open on my lap and the tears running down my face, I began to argue with the Holy Spirit. I said, "Really?! Really?! This is where You have me reading on the day after my husband was killed? Why couldn't I be reading in John, or the book of Psalms, or even Philippians?"

And Carol, you know what?! The Holy Spirit answered me and said, "Yes, Debby. I knew that Steve would be going to heaven on April 30, 2005, and I planned strategically for you to read in this place. I wanted to remind you that people are important to God and that Steve has been an important part of My plan at his moment in history."

Debby said she then wiped away her tears and continued to read:

And Cush begat Nimrod: he began to be mighty upon the earth. And Mizraim begat Ludim, and Anamim, and Lehabim, and Naphtuhim.   —1 Chronicles 1:10–11 KJV

Debby told me that she loved the Bible so much that now, even in her human grief, she had even fallen in love with the "begats."

Heart Inspection
What passage of Scripture has ministered to you during a time of pain or grief? Write it out below.

_____

_____

Heartfelt Prayer

Jesus, You are my best friend, my constant companion, and my comforter in times of grief. Today, I thank You for the power found in Your Word and the knowledge that not a single sentence is wasted or unnecessary. In Your name, I pray. Amen.

Eternal Words
_____

> *My soul weeps because of grief; strengthen me according to Your word.* —Psalm 119:28

_____

Reading the Blueprint
Read Psalm 119:73–104.

Your Highest Treasure

The Word of God has amazing cleansing power and absolute protective power in our lives. If you struggle with a certain sin, perhaps what you need is more of the Bible inside of you!

I have treasured Your word in my heart, so that I may not sin against You. —Psalm 119:11

Have you made the Word of God your highest treasure? Do you quote Scripture verses to yourself all day long? When you are standing in line at the grocery store, are you thinking about a particular verse in the Bible or about your daily frustrations? When you are waiting for your appointment at the doctor's office, are you playing games on your phone or are you internally quoting a few of your favorite Bible verses?

If you have hidden the Word of God in your heart, you have expertly installed a high-powered security system guaranteed to keep out any sin that threatens to steal your joy or hold you in bondage. If you choose a Scripture to memorize every week, by the end of the year, you will have fifty-two amazing spiritual weapons in your armament!

You are already clean because of the word which I have spoken to you. —John 15:3

Just as Christ also loved the church and gave Himself up for her, so that He might sanctify her, having cleansed her by the washing of water with the word. —Ephesians 5:25–26

Not only will God's miraculous Word keep you from sin, it will also cleanse you from sins you have committed in the past. The Bible will wash the drudge of sin and compromise out of your heart. The Word of God will wash away bitterness, impatience, and addictive behavior; it will restore your heart, launder your brain, and purify your soul. Nothing else can do what the Word of God is able to do!

The Bible has a miracle on every page, and it holds power in every single written word. It is able to put what my grandmother used to call a "spit shine" on the deepest and darkest parts of your life. The Word of God partners with the blood of Calvary to make you as white as snow!

Though your sins are as scarlet, they shall become as white as snow.

—Isaiah 1:18

The wonder of the Word of God is that it is able to clean out bad attitudes, negativity, and harmful behaviors faster than you can say, "I'm clean!"

Heart Inspection

What is the one sin that you deal with most often?

_____

_____

Have you asked for forgiveness for that sin?

_____

_____

Have you asked the Lord to give you the power to fight against that particular sin?

_____

_____

Heartfelt Prayer

Sweet Jesus, today I thank You that Your Word empowers me to stand strongly against sin and compromise. I also want to thank You that the Bible cleanses me from my sin and makes me as white as snow! In Jesus's name, I pray. Amen.

Eternal Words

Purify me with hyssop, and I will be clean; cleanse me, and I will be whiter than snow. —Psalm 51:7

Reading the Blueprint

Read Psalm 119:105–128.

Thinking Like God Thinks

The Word of God is not only your lifetime blueprint, but also a trust-worthy and astounding GPS. The Bible is able to give direction when you are headed the wrong way in life and clear a pathway when you feel that you are in the wilderness. The Bible is able to guide you out of dense dis-appointment and will ease the confusion when you simply don't know what to do next!

By your words I can see where I'm going; they throw a beam of light on my dark path. I've committed myself and I'll never turn back from living by your righteous order. Everything's falling apart on me, God; put me together again with your Word.
—Psalm 119:105–107 MSG

The Bible is God's way of giving His children direction while we are living on the *time side* of eternity. He knew that we, as frail human beings, would need assistance in order to make wise decisions and think like He thinks because He is our omniscient Father. The Bible has always been God's incredible plan to leave an indelible and deliberate mark upon the lives of His dear children. As you study the Bible, you will discover that you are making better decisions and you are thinking more clearly on the confusing days of life!

The best definition of the word "wisdom" that I have ever encoun-tered is this: "Wisdom is thinking like God thinks." If you want wisdom, which is thinking the very thoughts of God, then you must read the Word of God diligently. As you get to know God and His perfect character through the reading of His Word, you will discover that the attributes of God are infiltrating your life as well! What a wonder!

Your testimonies also are my delight; they are my advisers.
—Psalm 119:24

The best advice you will ever receive is found on the pages of Scripture; the most trusted counselor you could ever submit yourself to is the Word of God. If you take the advice of the culture, you will fall back into old sinful patterns and unhealthy thought processes. However, if you attach yourself to the Word of God and allow the Word to accomplish a deep, penetrating work in your life, you will discover a wisdom that is hidden to many.

I have more insight than all my teachers, for Your testimonies are my meditation. —Psalm 119:99

Heart Inspection

In what area of your life do you need wisdom?

Do you know of a Scripture verse that applies to this area?

Do you believe that it is possible to "think like God thinks"? Why or why not?

Heartfelt Prayer

Father God, I want to think like You think! I ask today that You would give me Your wisdom as I travel through life. I declare that I don't want my own way, but I want Your will and Your way! In Jesus's name, I pray. Amen.

Eternal Words

So teach us to number our days, that we may present to You a heart of wisdom. —Psalm 90:12

Reading the Blueprint

Read Psalm 119:129–152.

Never-Ending Supply of Power

When you are weak, you need to read your Bible. When you are in a battle, you need to arm yourself with the Word of God. When you are desperate for God to intervene in your life with His goodness, you need to bury yourself in the Bible!

If you ever find yourself in a weakened position in life (which you surely will), your first response should be to open the Bible and strengthen yourself from its never-ending supply of power.

My sad life's dilapidated, a falling-down barn; build me up again by your Word. Barricade the road that goes Nowhere; grace me with your clear revelation. I choose the true road to Somewhere, I post your road signs at every curve and corner. I grasp and cling to whatever you tell me; GOD, don't let me down! I'll run the course you lay out for me if you'll just show me how. —Psalm 119:28–32 MSG

Have you ever gone to the gym and expected to see instant results in your abs, your quads, or your glutes? Of course not! You know that exercising is a process and that if you remain consistent in lifting weights, dancing, cycling, aerobics, or running, then, eventually, your body will take on a new, improved shape. And so it is with reading the Word of God—it takes tenacity.

As you diligently apply yourself to studying the Word, the process will begin to become visible in your life. You will wonder why you don't get frustrated with that nosey girl at work anymore. What happened to you? The Word happened to you! You will wonder how you can be patient with your sister who complains all the time. What happened to you? The Word of God happened to you!

When you find yourself in a battle in life, you often might react out of emotions and even falsely believe that an emotional reaction is the preferred way to fight. You might fight back with anger, frustration, or gossip. Perhaps you defend yourself by eating chocolate, by spending money, or by giving someone the silent treatment. I must tell you that you will never win a battle in life if you fight back with your emotions! Your battle technique needs immediate improvement!

> *And take the helmet of salvation and the sword of the Spirit, which is the word of God.* —Ephesians 6:17

When you apply the power of the Word of God to every battle that comes your way, it will be an indispensable weapon in your arsenal. Find a fighting Scripture and then declare it, share it, pray it, memorize it, and sing it! In the midst of conflict of any kind at all, go to the Word as your first weapon of defense.

Do you realize that as you hide God's Word in your heart, it will position you for an extraordinary blessing? It's true! A blessing or two is coming your way as you delight yourself in the Bible!

> *Blessed is the person who does not walk in the counsel of the wicked, nor stand in the path of sinners, nor sit in the seat of scoffers! But his delight is in the Law of the LORD, and on His Law he meditates day and night.* —Psalm 1:1–2

Heart Inspection

What does it mean to "strengthen yourself in the Lord" in a practical sense?

_____

_____

How do you generally fight your battles in life?

_____

_____

What does it mean to meditate on the Word of God?

_____

_____

Heartfelt Prayer

Lord Jesus, I need You. I need You to fight my battles and to give me strength. I can't do life without You, dear Father. I choose You and I choose Your Word today and every day. In Jesus's name, I pray. Amen.

Eternal Words

I have inherited Your testimonies forever, for they are the joy of my heart. I have inclined my heart to perform Your statutes forever, even to the end. —Psalm 119:111–112

Reading the Blueprint

Read Psalm 119:153–176.

Part Three:
Insulation – The Love of God

The greatest honor we can give Almighty God is to live gladly because of the knowledge of His love.
—Julian of Norwich

It's time to insulate your heart with the love of God. As you enclose your doubts, your insecurities, and your nagging questions in the unending, extravagant love of the Father, you will discover that your heart will be safe and warm during the vicious days of life. *You are loved*—and there is nothing that you can do about it!

A Snug Little Home

My husband Craig and I lived in Buffalo, New York, in the 1980s. We were the proud, happy parents of two little boys. We were living on a pastor's salary and never had an abundance of money. We could afford a home…but believe me when I say that it was far from a *dream* home. We bought a classic fixer-upper that we never fixed up!

The only bathroom in the sad little house boasted an old-fashioned, claw-foot tub, which sounds very romantic and Victorian. However, all of the enamel on the inside was chipped off!

The washer and dryer were located in the basement, so as a young mom, I was down there often amidst the cobwebs, illuminated by one single lightbulb hanging from the ceiling. Did I mention that it was a dirt cellar to which you descended on a flight of rickety old wooden stairs that had no handrail?

One of the best things about this home is that it was small—miniature really. It only housed two bedrooms and one small bathroom. Craig and I thought, "Good! The heating bills will be low in the dead of winter in this tiny home!"

We had stretched ourselves financially with this fixer-upper and barely had enough income to pay the monthly mortgage. We were just scraping by from paycheck to paycheck, as most young families do.

When the winter of 1983-84 hit our pocketbooks with blizzard-like force, we were in shock, and it wasn't because of the fierce weather. Our heating bills were significantly higher than our mortgage! Our home was no better than a tent; the wind blew in around the windows and the heat blew out around the doors.

The next summer, Craig and my handyman father blew insulation into our home. The process was arduous, but they did it together in a week's time. They drilled small, round holes into the outside of the house every eighteen inches and then used a blower to blow insulation into every nook and cranny.

The following winter, our house was so snug that I was actually too hot every day of the long, frigid season. Our heating bills diminished drastically, the family was much more comfortable, and life was pleasurable even in the middle of another epic winter. When I was living in my snug, little home, I was blissfully unaware of the temperature outside my doors. I could see what was happening outside the tall windows, but I couldn't feel it because I lived in a home with adequate insulation.

What is the insulation of your life? What enables you to stay comfortable and even peaceful during the wailing storms around you? What is it that allows you to observe what is happening in your circumstances yet not be affected by them? What keeps the warmth of His presence inside your heart so that it doesn't escape into the atmosphere that is pushing in around you?

Most of us walk through life without allowing the Lord to fill the holes in our heart with His trustworthy insulation. He longs to fill the holes in your heart with the knowledge of His eternal, dynamic, and unconditional love for you. If you realized how deeply He loves you, the storms of life would not impact you to such a profound degree.

You are loved, dear one! You are loved by God—and there is nothing you can do about it!

Heart Inspection

How would you describe God's love for you in one word?

_____

_____

How would you describe your love for God in one word?

_____

_____

Does the love of the Father ever change toward His children?

_____

_____

Heartfelt Prayer

Jesus, thank You for Your unending love toward me. Would You teach me how to understand Your love and walk in it? In Jesus's name, I pray. Amen.

Eternal Words

> *See how great a love the Father has given us, that we would be called children of God; and in fact we are.* —1 John 3:1

Love Letter

Read Ephesians 2:1–10.

DAY 16

Nothing You Can Do About It!

For this reason I bend my knees before the Father, from whom every family in heaven and on earth derives its name, that He would grant you, according to the riches of His glory, to be strengthened with power through His Spirit in the inner self, so that Christ may dwell in your hearts through faith; and that you, being rooted and grounded in love, may be able to comprehend with all the saints what is the width and length and height and depth, and to know the love of Christ which surpasses knowledge, that you may be filled to all the fullness of God.
—Ephesians 3:14–19

Paul, the scholar and the leading voice for Christ in the early church, passionately informed the church at Ephesus that there was a driving issue that was compelling him to his knees on their behalf. There was a matter of utmost importance that constrained Paul to pray with every ounce of his strength for those under his watch.

Theologians believe that Paul was not merely bowing his knees, but that he was prostrating himself on the floor of the prison cell as he prayed for his brothers and sisters in Christ. The traditional Jewish position of prayer was standing with the hands stretched out and the palms facing upward. However, Paul's prayer for the early church, and therefore for us, was so intense that he prostrated himself to God almost in an agony of entreaty.

He longed for the early, persecuted church to know that there was only one way to obtain strength from the Holy Spirit and only one way to embrace Christ in their hearts. This one way was by knowing, in the deepest parts of the human soul, the love of Christ.

Do you know the love of Christ? Have you been able to wrap your heart around the eternal concept of the love of God? God's love is a gift and you can either choose to receive it or not. The fact that you might not choose to receive it in its full, lavish manner doesn't change the fact that He loves you.

My husband Craig has a friend who is a pastor and comrade in the faith. This committed young man has more pigment in his skin than Craig does and yet they are true brothers. D'Mott texts Craig often with these words: "I love you, brother, and there is nothing that you can do about it!"

Not only did Jesus come to this world as an infant, but He poured out His love in service to us as a Man. He healed the sick, raised the dead, comforted the lonely, fed the hungry, confronted the sinner, and prayed to His Father.

Then, His love was made visible and even tangible when He died for you and for me. Has anyone other than Christ ever died for you? His love for you is relentless and eternal. Your status in life makes no difference to God's love for you. He loves you completely—and there is nothing you can do about it.

Heart Inspection

What is the one issue that drives you to your knees in prayer?

What posture do you take when you pray? Do you sit? Stand? Kneel? Lie face down?

Is there anything you could *do* to make God love you more?

Is there anything you could *do* to make God love you less?

Heartfelt Prayer

Jesus, I come to You today as a woman who desperately wants to be loved. Thank You for Your assurance of Your love toward me. Help me to know Your love in greater ways. In Jesus's name, I pray. Amen.

Eternal Words

The LORD your God is in your midst, a victorious warrior. He will rejoice over you with joy, He will be quiet in His love, He will rejoice over you with shouts of joy. —Zephaniah 3:17

Love Letter

Read 1 Corinthians 13.

Rooted and Grounded

We will be spending more time on the Scripture that we read yesterday. I have found this passage to be rich in its intent and meaning concerning the powerful, never-diminishing, astonishing love of God! As you reread these verses today, ask the Holy Spirit to give you a fresh revelation of the love of God.

For this reason I bend my knees before the Father, from whom every family in heaven and on earth derives its name, that He would grant you, according to the riches of His glory, to be strengthened with power through His Spirit in the inner self, so that Christ may dwell in your hearts through faith; and that you, being rooted and grounded in love, may be able to comprehend with all the saints what is the width and length and height and depth, and to know the love of Christ which surpasses knowledge, that you may be filled to all the fullness of God. —Ephesians 3:14–19

Paul was endeavoring to describe something indescribable in these verses. It was so formidable for Paul to communicate what the Holy Spirit had shown him about the love of the Father that he mixed metaphors. He utilized both an agricultural term and a building term in his attempt to describe the love of God.

Paul reminds us that we are *"rooted"* in God's love, an agricultural phrase. God's love is nourishing, and our fragile roots are meant to burrow deeply into the soil of God's never-ending and all-encompassing love. Our only chance of growing in faith is to be nurtured and fed by His rich love.

Secondly, Paul uses the building term *"grounded"* or *"established"* (NIV). God's love builds a solid foundation in our temporary lives. It is God's love that offers stability and a depth of purpose and meaning.

Whether you are in the growing business or the building business, the starting point for both is the same place: God loves you! He loves you just the way you are! It is impossible for you to build anything that is not built upon the love of God. It is preposterous to think that you will grow anything that is not rooted in God's great love for you.

Often, we may be unable to relate to the love of God because we are incapable of loving the way He does. We try to *humanize* the holy and eternal love of God. But our love is temporary and conditional; God's love is eternal and unlimited, with no strings attached. We, as human beings, may grow tired of loving the same person, and so we get frustrated and move on. If someone disappoints us, we selfishly take part of our love back. If someone angers us, we withhold the warmth and affection of our love toward that annoying person.

God's love isn't like our love—He doesn't hold back based upon the actions of His beloved children. He never changes His mind based upon disappointment. He never moves on to someone more lovable when He is frustrated with us. Never!

He loves you—and there is nothing you can do about it!

Heart Inspection

Is there someone from whom you are withholding love? How can you show God's love to this person?

_____

_____

What does it mean to you to be *"rooted and grounded"* in God's love?

_____

_____

Heartfelt Prayer

Jesus, teach me to love like You love. Give me an expansive, unconditional love for my family and friends. In Jesus's name, I pray. Amen.

Eternal Words

May the Lord direct your hearts to the love of God and to the perseverance of Christ. —2 Thessalonians 3:5

Love Letter

Read John 14.

No Boundaries

Let's go digging for gold one more time in the passage that Paul wrote from his imprisonment in Rome. Can you even imagine that a man in the confines of an ancient prison would pen these words filled with the treasure of the ages?

So that Christ may dwell in your hearts through faith; and that you, being rooted and grounded in love, may be able to comprehend with all the saints what is the width and length and height and depth, and to know the love of Christ which surpasses knowledge, that you may be filled to all the fullness of God. —Ephesians 3:17–19

Paul inserted more architectural terminology in his description of the love of God as he exalts, *"That you…may be able to comprehend with all the saints what is the width and length and height and depth."* Paul used terms that are also used when plotting a building. He asserts that the love of Christ cannot be measured.

Prior to Calvary, there was no way that a human could fully enjoy the love of God. We simply weren't good enough to penetrate the boundaries of God's love. However, when Jesus died on the cross, He took God's love for sinners outside of any constraints or boundaries. In a single, miraculous moment, the dividing line that was between you and the love of God was obliterated. Jesus made a way for you to access His love!

There is no longer a boundary line that denies your entrance into the love of God. It is a love that surpasses all depths, all heights, all lengths, and all widths. There are no boundaries! There is no end to His love for you!

It is extremely difficult to understand this boundless love because our love has boundaries. Even our love for those we hold most dear—our spouse, our children, our parents—has limitations. If we do not comprehend God's love for us, our love for others will remain "BC," or before the cross. We will love when we feel like it and when people behave in ways we think they should. We will choose to love others when we are not frustrated with their behavior and when they haven't done anything foolish this month. That type of love is "BC" love—before the cross.

But if you have experienced the love and power of the cross, you will die to self and you will love with the love of the cross. To a large degree, your emotional reactions must decline; you must stop demanding that your feelings take preeminence. The greatest mistake that we make in our human relationships is that we falsely believe that God loves *like us* when we are called to love *like Him*!

The Father loves you so much that He sent His only Son to die for you—and there is nothing you can do about it!

Heart Inspection

Have you tried to *earn* the love of God in your life? If so, how?

_____

_____

What is your definition of the phrase "human love"?

_____

_____

What is your definition of God's love?

_____

_____

Heartfelt Prayer

Dear Jesus, I want to love like You love. Would You do a miracle in my heart today and give me the power and capacity to love more like You do? In the name of Jesus, I pray. Amen.

Eternal Words

For I am convinced that neither death, nor life, nor angels, nor principalities, nor things present, nor things to come, nor powers, nor height, nor depth, nor any other created thing will be able to separate us from the love of God that is in Christ Jesus our Lord.

—Romans 8:38–39

Love Letter

Read John 15.

Inexhaustible Abundance

Napoleon's troops opened a prison that had been used during the Spanish Inquisition in the late 1400s. They discovered the remains of a prisoner who had been incarcerated for his faith nearly 350 years earlier. His body had long since decayed in the underground dungeon in which it was found.

A thick, heavy metal chain was still fastened around his anklebone that was now lifeless and devoid of skin, flesh, and blood. But this prisoner, although he had been dead for centuries, was speaking still. This tethered man had left a witness. Although we will never know his name, his heart was still beating for Christ.

The words of Paul, in the book of Ephesians, had made a difference in this martyr's life. On the wall of his small, dismal cell, this faithful soldier of Jesus Christ had scratched a rough cross with four words surrounding it in Spanish. Above the cross was the Spanish word for "height" and below it was the word for "depth." The word for "length" was to the right of the chiseled cross and to the left was the word for "width."

That you...may be able to comprehend with all the saints what is the width and length and height and depth, and to know the love of Christ which surpasses knowledge, that you may be filled to all the fullness of God. —Ephesians 3:17–19

The only way to measure the love of Christ is by the cross of Calvary. The *"width"* of His love implies that it goes to the utmost corners of the earth; the *"length"* communicates that it is as long as it is wide. How wide is the love of Christ? It goes to the ends of the earth!

Every other time that the particular word *"height"* is used in the New Testament, it refers to heaven. The love of Christ is as high as heaven!

The *"depth"* of Christ's love is ours in an inexhaustible abundance. We carry within us an immense amount of love to envelop our human souls while we live on Earth. We are the recipients of a love so extravagant and so immeasurable that it changes the way we talk, the way we think, the way we treat others, and the way we live.

Jesus stopped breathing so that you would be breathless at His love. His heart stopped beating so that your heartbeat would quicken at the very thought of His love. He died so that you could live in His love.

Understanding the love of Christ will bring nourishment for your entire life, and it will give you a solid foundation upon which to build a life. When you *know* the love of Christ, you will know something that surpasses knowledge! Paul used the word for "know" that means to experience intimately. We must go beyond understanding the love of God with our minds to experiencing it personally. We are invited to be in a love relationship with God Himself.

The Jesus who died on the cross of Calvary loves you—and there is nothing you can do about it!

Heart Inspection

How do you experience the love of God in a practical sense?

_____

_____

What are you an expert at?

_____

_____

Is it possible to be an expert at knowing the love of God?

_____

_____

Heartfelt Prayer

Jesus, I want to know You in Your glory and in Your love. Help me to fall in love with You more deeply every day that I am alive. In Jesus's name, I pray. Amen.

Eternal Words

May the Lord direct your hearts to the love of God and to the perseverance of Christ. —2 Thessalonians 3:5

Love Letter

Read Psalm 147.

The Bible Tells Me So

Perhaps the moment that we truly know the love of God in its fullness and power is when we apply the love of God to our relationships with others. Maybe we will finally understand the love of God when we begin to act like God acts and love like God loves.

Beloved, let's love one another; for love is from God, and everyone who loves has been born of God and knows God. The one who does not love does not know God, because God is love. —1 John 4:7–8

When we overlook the disappointing behavior of others and when we rise above the frustrations, the mess, and the immaturity and love them, these are the exciting moments when our hearts are beating in sync with the Father's love.

If I could just share one important addendum with you, it would be this: the Father doesn't want you to be abused physically or emotionally. He just wants you to be unselfish. Loving like God loves doesn't mean that we are called to sacrifice our sanity; however, He always calls us to sacrifice our selfishness.

In most of our relationships, we are called to extravagantly love, not because someone earned it or deserved it, but because we are loved completely by God so we are able to love others.

But because of his great love for us, God, who is rich in mercy, made us alive with Christ even when we were dead in transgressions—it is by grace you have been saved. —Ephesians 2:4–5 NIV

At the worst moment of your life, God was totally, passionately, and undeniably head over heels in love with you. Your actions, failures, and sin nature don't change Him or His love because His love is not based upon performance but it is based intrinsically upon who He is.

Karl Barth was one of the most esteemed thinkers of the twentieth century, and many religious leaders believe that he was the greatest theologian since the apostle Paul. Barth stood against Hitler before World

War II and wrote volumes of theology based on the Word of God. Barth painstakingly wrote a thirteen-volume work that was six million words long entitled *Church Dogmatics*.

Once, a young seminary student asked Barth if he could sum up what was most important about his life's work and theology in just a few words. The audience gasped at the impertinent question. Barth thought for just a moment. Then he smiled and said, "Yes, in the words of a song my mother used to sing to me, 'Jesus loves me, this I know, for the Bible tells me so.'"

In Barth's esteemed opinion, the love of Jesus was more important than six million words of theology. I am sure that Barth would agree: Jesus loves you—and there is absolutely nothing you can do about it!

Heart Inspection

Is there a relationship that you need to take a break from because it is abusive either emotionally or physically?

When have you felt most loved by God?

When do you most need God's love?

Heartfelt Prayer

Jesus, help me to love people who disagree with me and people who are at their worst. Give me wisdom in all of my relationships. Thank You, Father God. In Jesus's name, I pray. Amen.

Eternal Words

Beloved, if God so loved us, we also ought to love one another.
—1 John 4:11

Love Letter

Read Ephesians 1.

Daddy God

Can we look back for just a moment? Let's re-visit the Scripture that began our fascinating journey into experiencing the love of God.

For this reason I bend my knees before the Father, from whom every family in heaven and on earth derives its name, that He would grant you, according to the riches of His glory, to be strengthened with power through His Spirit in the inner self, so that Christ may dwell in your hearts through faith; and that you, being rooted and grounded in love, may be able to comprehend with all the saints what is the width and length and height and depth, and to know the love of Christ which surpasses knowledge, that you may be filled to all the fullness of God. —Ephesians 3:14–19

Right after Paul informed the church at Ephesus that he was praying for them, he reminded them to whom he would be praying—the Father.

There are two distinct words for "father" in Greek, and they offer a wide range of meaning. There is the word that is most accurately translated as "paternity" and is used in a purely physical sense of the word. It can actually be used to describe a father who has never seen or spoken with his child. When men used the word "father" before Jesus came, it was in this sense of paternity.

The second word for "father" holds all of the intimacy, love, fellowship, and care that the word "daddy" in English conveys.

In the Old Testament, God was the Person to whom access was forbidden; in the New Testament, we are invited to run boldly into His presence. We can now do this because He is our Daddy.

A story is told of a little boy in England whose father, in the early years of the twentieth century, was promoted to the exalted rank of brigadier in the queen's army. When the small child heard the news, he was silent for just a minute and then inquired, "Do you think he will mind if I still call him 'Daddy'"?

My friend, you get to call Him Daddy! Run into His loving arms with reckless abandon. Don't allow your failures, shortcomings, or doubts to hold you at arm's length with the One who knows you best and loves you most.

The enemy has lied to women about the love of God. You mistakenly believe that God couldn't possibly love you because of your weight, your past sin, your marital status, or your habits. You might feel as if you are not good enough for God to love you because you have yelled at your children, you are in debt, or you are inclined to fantasize. Be assured today that it's not that God merely acts lovingly or talks lovingly, but that He *is* Love! Love is the only way that the Father knows to be; He is not able to be unkind, to act selfishly, or to ignore His children. Those behavior patterns are outside of the height, the depth, the length, and the width of His love for you.

God loves you—and there is absolutely nothing that you can do about it!

Heart Inspection

What are some of the issues in life that have convinced you that you are not worthy of God's love for you?

_____

_____

What was your relationship like with your earthly father?

_____

_____

How has your relationship with your earthly father impacted the way you view God's love?

_____

_____

Heartfelt Prayer

Daddy, I come to You today in the loving name of Jesus and I run boldly into Your arms. Thank You that I can throw my cares upon You because You care for me. In Jesus's name, I pray. Amen.

Eternal Words

Cast all your anxiety on him because he cares for you.

—1 Peter 5:7 NIV

Love Letter

Read Colossians 1.

Part Four:
Open the Windows – Prayer

To be a Christian without prayer is no more possible
than to be alive without breathing.
—Martin Luther

If you long to live fully for Christ, then you will pray. It is both
your destiny and your delight. If you want to open your heart
to the needs of others, you must make a daily commitment to
prayer. When you pray, not only are the windows of your heart
opened to all that God has for you, but the windows of heaven
are open over your life as well. You will feel the fresh breeze of the
Holy Spirit enter in and rejuvenate you as you pray for others.

Throw Open Your Heart

There is nothing like a breath of fresh air after the stale, cold, and cramped days of winter! How invigorating, on the first day of spring, to throw open the windows and enthusiastically welcome sunshine, the sweet fragrance of new growth, and an exhilarating breeze into one's home.

Prayer is the way in which we are spiritually able to bring new life, vivid atmosphere, and revived hope into the heart that we call home. When you open your heart through the windows of prayer, you will be offered a view of life that is filled with unmatched possibilities and uncommon assignments. As you throw wide the shutters and drink in the view of opportunity in God's kingdom, your prayer life will spring into being and will be filled with power and with promise.

How wonderful that God would ask us, as fallible human beings, to partner with Him in filling the world with His hope! The partnership that God offers is accompanied by the personal invitation to pray.

How marvelous that the Father risks our novice help in ushering in His kingdom to earth! He allows us the opportunity to pick up the shovel of prayer and begin digging the foundation of kingdom living while in the confines of time.

How miraculous to believe that our prayers make a difference in the lives of those whom we love!

> To pray is to enter the treasure-house of God and to gather riches
> out of an inexhaustible storehouse.   —Charles Spurgeon

Throw open the windows of your heart today and expose your life to the breeze of the Holy Spirit. As the Holy Spirit rushes into the winter places of your heart, you will experience burgeoning life and sprouting joy as never before. The Holy Spirit will reward you with new assignments and with unique purpose as you spend time in prayer. The Holy Spirit will empower you to accomplish so much more than you ever could on your own.

There has never been a better day than today to offer your life in the pursuit of prayer. There has never been a more appropriate moment than now to respond to the Father's summons to join Him in making a mark on human history.

Throw open your heart and pray!

Heart Inspection

What excites you about spending time in prayer?

_____

_____

Who has prayed for you along your life's journey? Have you taken the time to thank that person?

_____

_____

What is one miracle that you have experienced in your lifetime? Tell someone about it this week. It will be an encouragement to them!

_____

_____

Heartfelt Prayer

> Jesus, today I open the windows of my heart and I enter into a divine partnership of prayer with You! Father, give me assignments in prayer to which I can commit myself. Give me the power of the Holy Spirit to accomplish Your purposes. In Jesus's name, I pray. Amen.

Eternal Words

> *Therefore, confess your sins to one another, and pray for one another so that you may be healed. A prayer of a righteous person, when it is brought about, can accomplish much.* —James 5:16

Enjoying the View

Read 2 Chronicles 7:12–16.

Wear God Out

When Jesus desired to teach His disciples the importance of persistent and enduring prayer, He told them a story about a judge and a widow.

> *Now He was telling them a parable to show that at all times they ought to pray and not become discouraged.*   —Luke 18:1

The judge was a godless man who didn't even like people! (See Luke 18:2.) Can you imagine a judge like that?! The widow was in some type of legal battle, and she repeatedly came to this judge, asking for legal protection from her opponent.

> *For a while [the judge] was unwilling; but later he said to himself, "Even though I do not fear God nor respect any person, yet because this widow is bothering me, I will give her justice; otherwise by continually coming she will wear me out."*   —Luke 18:4–5

Now remember, Jesus told His disciples this story to show them that at all times, they ought to pray and not to lose heart!

I believe that Jesus is challenging believers of every generation to *wear Him out in prayer!* Is that even possible?! Is it possible to wear God out in prayer? I don't know, but I can tell you this: I will spend every day of my life and every breath in my lungs trying to do just that!

> It is not a matter of time so much as a matter of heart; if you have the heart to pray, you will find the time.   —Charles Spurgeon

Why worry when you can pray? Why do anything else when you have been given the power that only prayer provides? God has entrusted us with the vehicle by which we can change not only our own circumstances, but also impact the world. Prayer has the power to change people, circumstances, events, times, and even history!

Worry has no intrinsic power at all. Worry will never trump one circumstance, situation, or person! Worry actually entices you into a tenacious stronghold that will leave its ugly imprints on your mind and heart.

I have heard it said that when you worry, you are in agreement with Satan, who is the deceiver of believers.

You were not created for worry, but you were created for sweet communion with God on your knees in the prayer closet of your heart. One of the most marvelous aspects of prayer is that you can do it at anytime and anywhere!

Heart Inspection

How long do you spend in prayer each day? Be honest.

_____

_____

How long would you like to spend in prayer each day?

_____

_____

What is your one, central prayer request right now?

_____

_____

Heartfelt Prayer

Jesus, I want to pray. I want to spend time on my knees every day in prayer. Lord Jesus, would You create the deep longing in my heart to spend time with You in prayer? In Jesus's name, I pray. Amen.

Eternal Words

Do not be anxious about anything, but in every situation, by prayer and petition, with thanksgiving, present your requests to God.
—Philippians 4:6 NIV

Enjoying the View

Read Luke 18:1–8 and Matthew 6:9–13.

People

There is a lovely secret hidden in the very fabric of our prayers for others; perhaps you have already discovered it! Words spoken in a passionate conversation rarely change the person who needs my advice or wisdom. However, when I pray to the Father rather than just pontificate with people, lasting change is accomplished.

The lingering truth is this: people can run from your words, but they can never escape the impact of your prayers! My strategy in dealing with difficult and fractious folks is to talk less and pray more. My approach when trying to get my adult children to see things from my point of view is to talk less and pray more. My system of marital bliss is to talk less and pray more. My policy in dealing with friends, coworkers, or family members is to talk less and pray more.

> When a Christian shuns fellowship with other Christians, the devil smiles. When he stops studying the Bible, the devil laughs. When he stops praying, the devil shouts for joy.
> —Corrie ten Boom

My prayer journal is tattered, worn, and stained with tears. It is also the most powerful book in my possession—except for my Bible, of course! On the pages of this beloved prayer ledger are written the names and the specific requests that I have brought into the throne room of God over the years. I have chronicled answered prayers, bona fide miracles, and fighting verses that have kept my voice in the throne room of the King. Do you have a prayer journal? It has helped me to be more consistent in daily prayer. Pray every day, my friend! Wear God out with your prayers! Journal your deepest requests, your unanswerable questions, and your greatest blessings.

> Some people think God does not like to be troubled with our constant coming and asking. The way to trouble God is not to come at all.
> —D. L. Moody

Resolve to be a prayer warrior that hell fears and heaven applauds!

Resolve to be a prayer warrior that Satan himself runs from when he hears you coming!

Resolve to be known for such a commitment to prayer that heaven taps you on the shoulder at all times of the day and night and then places a prayer request in your heart and mind.

Prayer should never be your last response—it should always be your first response! We are the first responders! We are the people of God who believe in the power of prayer!

I resolve to pray! Every day! Everywhere! At all times!

Heart Inspection

Do you have a prayer journal? If not, let me encourage you to choose one today.

_____

_____

Has God ever awakened you in the night for prayer? How did you respond?

_____

Is anything too difficult for the Lord? Be honest! What do you believe? Is anything too difficult for the Lord?

_____

_____

Heartfelt Prayer

Lord Jesus, I thank You that You hear me when I pray. I rejoice in the fact that my God inclines His ear to me as I call out to Him in prayer. Father, I confess today in Jesus's name that nothing, absolutely nothing, is too difficult for You. Amen.

Eternal Words

In the morning, LORD, You will hear my voice; in the morning I will present my prayer to You and be on the watch.   —Psalm 5:3

Enjoying the View

Read Psalm 66.

A Telling Question

"Devotion" is a powerful and substantive word, isn't it? The word comes with no ambiguities or gray areas; the eight letters that comprise the word *devotion* clearly state what it means.

Devotion is profound dedication, especially to religion, or an earnest attachment to a cause or a person.

Devote yourselves to prayer, keeping alert in it with an attitude of thanksgiving. —Colossians 4:2

To what or to whom are you devoted? It's a telling question, isn't it? Are you devoted to the acquisition of money or the advancement of your career? Some women are devoted to fashion, home improvement, or interior design, while others are devoted to education or prestige. I know some women who are devoted to travel, health and fitness, or food. I am unashamedly devoted to my children, my grandchildren, and my marriage.

Regardless of where your devotion is focused, I guarantee that you will indeed place most of your concentration and thought life on that single element in life that your heart has deemed of the utmost importance—your devotion.

Whatever you are sincerely devoted to, you will think about it day and night; it's likely your last thought at night before you lay your tired head on the pillow, and it is your first thought in the morning before your feet hit the floor. Whatever has captured the devotion of your heart, you assuredly make room for it in your life, and you likely push other interests and activities out of the way. You create time for your devotions, spend money on your devotions, and talk about your devotions to others.

Why cannot men find time for prayer? The only answer is because they do not love it. —Charles Spurgeon

Paul and the Holy Spirit, in the epistle to the believers at Colossae, commands this first-century church to be devoted to prayer. I have often wondered why God, in all of His infinite wisdom, called the body of Christ at every historical juncture to this particular devotion.

Why didn't Paul say, "Devote yourselves to fasting?"

Or why didn't the Holy Spirit whisper in Paul's ear, "Tell Christians from every future century to devote themselves to tithing?"

Now, certainly fasting and tithing are important disciplines in life, but the truth is that the Holy Spirit, through the pen of Paul, said this: *"Devote yourselves to prayer."*

Was it God's intent for every Christian to spend his or her life cloistered in a closet far away from the world and its influence? Were we never to engage in serving one another or encouraging one another face to face? Absolutely not!

God commands his faithful children to choose a devotion to prayer so that we can partner with Him in making a difference in the world. Never forget that history belongs to those who pray!

Heart Inspection

If you could pray for one current event right now, what would it be?

_____

_____

If you could pray for one nation right now, what nation would you pray for?

_____

_____

If you could pray for one world leader right now, who would you pray for?

_____

_____

Heartfelt Prayer

Jesus, fan the flame of devotion in my heart in the arena of prayer. I long to fall in love with You, and with Your people, on my knees in prayer. Thank You, Father, for the power that is mine when I pray. In Jesus's name, I pray. Amen.

Eternal Words

> Listen, LORD, to my prayer; and give Your attention to the sound of my pleading! —Psalm 86:6

Enjoying the View

Read Psalm 91.

DAY 26

Not an Option

Paul was writing to the church at Ephesus from a Roman prison cell. As Paul was contemplating how to encourage his fellow believers, his heart turned toward the importance of prayer. While Paul might have only believed that he was encouraging a certain group of people during a particular moment in church history, the Holy Spirit knew that Paul's encouragement would echo through the ages and help believers even in the twenty-first century to live valiantly and victoriously for the cause of Christ.

During Paul's imprisonment in Rome, it is likely that he was guarded continuously by a Roman soldier who was dressed in military gear. As Paul is bringing to a close the portion of Ephesians 6 known as *the full armor of God,*" he inserts one final piece of weaponry that he knew could do lethal havoc to the strategy of the enemy. What is this piece of weaponry? I believe that it is prayer.

> *With every prayer and request, pray at all times in the Spirit, and with this in view, be alert with all perseverance and every request for all the saints.* —Ephesians 6:18

Prayer is our heavy, effective weapon of warfare that will do great damage to the tactics of the enemy. Paul calls us to pray at all times. This means that anytime you have a chance to pray, you should pray. You should negate other things from your schedule and spend time with the Father in prayer. Every opportunity that you can possibly pray, you should pray! No matter where you are or what you are doing, take the time to pray. Seize time for prayer! When you are tempted to give time to other things such as games on your phone, scrolling through social media, or binging on television, pray instead.

Prayer was never meant to be optional for a believer in Jesus Christ. Prayer is not a mere possibility, but it is an assured requirement. Prayer is not one option on a list of multiple choice answers, but it is the only answer! Prayer is not a fleeting suggestion, but it is a command to the believer in Jesus Christ.

No time to pray? Had you time to dress? If you had purposed to pray, you would have prayed. —Charles Spurgeon

The power of prayer is absolutely atomic and is able to blast to smithereens in one instant the plans and deception of the enemy. Prayer is the strongest problem-solving power available to humanity, and prayer is the winning blow! Without prayer, a believer is doomed to a life of uncertainty, futile wishing, and untouched power; with prayer, a believer is able to change the course of history and overwhelmingly triumph in Jesus's name!

Heart Inspection
Why do you believe that so many Christians don't make time for prayer?

_____

_____

What are some of the things that have distracted you from spending time in prayer?

_____

_____

Do you view prayer as a last resort or as a first response?

_____

_____

Heartfelt Prayer

Lord Jesus, forgive me for ignoring the power that You have given to me in prayer. Today I open the windows of my heart for a fresh breeze of the Holy Spirit. Fill my life with the desire to pray for others. In Jesus's name, I pray. Amen.

Eternal Words

Incline Your ear, LORD, and answer me; for I am afflicted and needy. —Psalm 86:1

Enjoying the View
Read Ephesians 1:15–21.

Persevering Prayer

I'll admit it, I can be a wimp in the prayer closet. How about you? I often "throw in" my prayer towel long before I see a result or prior to making a difference. Oh, I might remember to utter a prayerful sentence here and there when I am in the shower or doing the dishes, but when it comes to prolonged and determined prayer, I give up. I give in.

> *With every prayer and request, pray at all times in the Spirit, and with this in view, be alert **with all perseverance** and every request for all the saints.* —Ephesians 6:18

In this rich verse, Paul not only calls believers to pray all the time, but he also gives us instructions on exactly *how* to pray. We are required, by the unction of the Holy Spirit, to pray *"with all perseverance."*

This is the only time that the word "perseverance" is used in the New Testament. It is translated as "to give unremitting care to a thing; to show one's self courageous for; to continue all the time; to persevere and not to faint."

It amazes this feeble prayer warrior that the word "perseverance" is only used in relationship to prayer. I wonder if the Holy Spirit knew that people like me were likely to walk away from prayer in pursuit of other interests.

Open the windows of your heart, my friend. Don't ever close those glorious windows again!

Prayer can never be in excess.   —Charles Spurgeon

If you are going to be persistent and consistent in any spiritual discipline, let it be prayer.

If you are going to be courageous and bold about any choice in life, let it be in the arena of prayer.

It has been said that you don't need to be good at prayer to get the job done; you just need to mean it. So pray on with a sincere heart and a strong faith.

Perhaps the singular reason why the enemy tries so diligently to distract us from prayer is because he knows the power that has been given to us when we pray the simplest of human prayers. If you are wondering how to pray today, any one of these short but wise prayers will get the job done:

"Lord! Help me!"

"Jesus! I need You!"

"Father, forgive me!"

"Lord, thank You!"

Heart Inspection

What are some of the other interests or hobbies in your life that you have been able to show perseverance in?

Why have you been able to persevere in those interests?

What does it mean to you to persevere?

Heartfelt Prayer

Oh, dear Jesus! How I long to persevere in the arena of prayer! Give me courage and boldness as I enter Your throne room. Give me grace to pray for others. In Jesus's matchless name, I pray. Amen.

Eternal Words

Hear my prayer, LORD, listen to my pleadings! Answer me in Your faithfulness, in Your righteousness! —Psalm 143:1

Enjoying the View

Read Daniel 9:3–23.

A Purposeful, Peaceful, Powerful Place

But as for you, when you pray, go into your inner room,
close your door, and pray to your Father who is in secret;
and your Father who sees what is done in secret will reward you.
—Matthew 6:6

Tucked away in the bowels of your heart is a place that only you and God are invited to enter. It is a quiet haven of unspoken purpose, and it is rich with the peace that surpasses understanding. The inexpressible peace that rules and reigns in your heart is preeminent, yet still your heart is where battles are fought and where victories are won.

In this solitary place, innermost secrets are revealed and desires are delicately whispered. It is here that righteousness is imputed and birthright is demanded!

This inconspicuous room in your heart hosts a solitary high-back chair that is accompanied only by a nightstand on which sits a candle whose wick burns brightly. A Bible and a well-worn prayer journal are the only two other added adornments.

The rug, lying humbly in front of the chair, boasts of two worn spots on which a nameless prayer warrior has spent nights on her knees in battle.

The walls are barren in the prayer closet of one's heart because no decorations are necessary in this powerful yet hidden room. Creature comforts are efficiently ignored in this tucked away place, and no signs of extravagance or personality have been added.

Above all, let us be much alone with Jesus. —Charles Spurgeon

This room is all about spirit; it is the place where my spirit touches the Spirit of God. This room is where I reach up to heaven, while standing on my tiptoes, and stretch with every ounce of human energy. My loving Father reaches down, scoops me into His lap, and touches my humanity with His divinity. The touching of my spirit with His Spirit becomes an embrace that will last for all of eternity. The prayer closet of my heart is where my heart touches the heart of God and lingers in His presence.

When you have spent time with Jesus in the deepest places of your heart, you will discover that you have developed an audacious faith! You will verbalize the full confidence that God hears every word that you speak. We are invited to come into the throne room of the Creator of the universe fearlessly, confidently, and boldly! The Lord isn't interested in your doubts; instead, He longs to hear all about your incredible faith! You have been given power in the kingdom of God and you access this miraculous power through prayer and faith. So open wide the windows of your heart!

Therefore, let's approach the throne of grace with confidence, so that we may receive mercy and find grace for help at the time of our need.
—Hebrews 4:16

Heart Inspection
What is the one lasting lesson you have learned about prayer this week?

How will you change your prayer strategy based on this lesson?

Do you have a prayer partner?

Heartfelt Prayer

Jesus, would You teach me to pray? Would You align my will with Your greater plan? I concede all that I am and all that I have to Your kingdom purposes. In Jesus's name, I pray. Amen.

Eternal Words

Ask, and it will be given to you; seek, and you will find; knock, and it will be opened to you. For everyone who asks receives, and he who seeks finds, and to the one who knocks it will be opened.

—Matthew 7:7–8

Enjoying the View

Read Psalm 103.

Part Five:
The Heart of the Home – Worship

Isn't it a comfort to worship a God we cannot exaggerate?
—Francis Chan

Is your heart a place of worship? Have you filled every room of your heart with a contagious melody that cannot be silenced? If you long for your heart to be a place of lasting joy and ultimate peace, you will worship every day joyously with the saints of the ages.

DAY 29
The Atmosphere of Home

Every home carries with it an atmosphere—an odor, if you will—of the folks who reside under its protective roof. Some homes are filled with anger and animosity, while others are filled with laughter and a sweet confusion of all that a family should be. Stress, perfectionism, and even a cold silence compromise the heart of some homes.

I remember the indescribably precious times I walked into my mother-in-law's home; I drank in an expectant breath because I knew that I would get an exquisite whiff of gardenia perfume, my father-in-law's tobacco, and whatever was baking in the oven. The delightful essence of my in-laws' home always whispered, "Welcome home! You are exactly where you need to be!"

What is the atmosphere of your heart? Our hearts were designed to be a concert hall of grand worship and magnificent song! God created our hearts to break out into a rare melody when life is hard and praise Him even in the storm. The aroma of our hearts should be the fragrance that only worship offers.

The heart of your physical body is the place from which life flows, and it is the organ that stabilizes all other bodily functions. Without a healthy and active heart muscle, not much else will remain healthy in the body that God gave to you.

So it is with your spiritual heart. It will ensure that you are living an abundant life, and it will also stabilize all other earthly assignments and disciplines. Your spiritual heart was given to you so that you would create the sound that only you were born to produce. You were born to worship! You were created to give glory back to the One who created you!

Be filled with the Spirit, speaking to one another in psalms and hymns and spiritual songs, singing and making melody with your hearts to the Lord. —Ephesians 5:18–19

When people walk into the life of a believer in Jesus Christ, their first whiff should be the fragrant aroma of the symphony of praise that we were born to sing. You should be identified by the rich melody that comes from your life and from your heart. The people of your generation are waiting; they are listening intently to hear the song of your heart, and with the song comes the fragrance of heaven's wonder.

*For we are a **fragrance** of Christ to God among those who are being saved and among those who are perishing.* —2 Corinthians 2:15

The heart of your home is a song of absolute worship! What a wonderful way to live!

Heart Inspection

What is your first response to a difficult time in life?

What does it mean to make melody with your heart?

How is it possible to speak to one another *"in psalms and hymns and spiritual songs"?*

Heartfelt Prayer

Lord Jesus, thank You for filling my life with the glory of a song. Would You accept my worship today as a sacrifice? I praise You, Lord, for who You are. In Jesus's name, I pray. Amen.

Eternal Words

Let the word of Christ richly dwell within you, with all wisdom teaching and admonishing one another with psalms, hymns, and spiritual songs, singing with thankfulness in your hearts to God.
—Colossians 3:16

Reading the Lyrics

Read Psalm 100.

DAY 30
But Where Does It Come From?

It was wretchedly hot in North Carolina that summer. I drove a twelve-passenger Dodge Ram van in order to accommodate my five children, their friends, our family dog, and everyone's stuff. There was one problem with that spacious ark: it lacked air conditioning.

We were deep into July, the steamiest days of the year on anyone's calendar, and I had to run a multitude of errands that day. We would go to the grocery store, the post office, and the drug store, return overdue books to the library, and have the oil changed in our home on wheels. I only had the three younger children with me on this sticky day and had wisely "watered them up" before we commenced on the monotonous journey around town.

The McLeod quartet had been in the van for nearly two hours, when Jordan, my precocious six-year-old, informed me, "Mom, I need a drink!"

I had no extra money to buy three thirsty children drinks from the fast-food drive-through or from the drug store, so as a veteran mom, I decided to take the conversation in a different and creative direction.

"Oh! Jordan, does that mean you need to wet your whistle?" was my reflexive response.

"What does that mean, Mom? What does it mean to wet your whistle?" my miniature Einstein responded.

"Well, your whistle is made by your tongue, which is a muscle, and so when a person is thirsty, it means that they need to wet their whistle" was my seasoned reply. "Does that make sense to you?"

I was so proud of myself! I was buying myself time to finish my errands before my three children had a meltdown due to the heat and their thirst.

"Well, if your whistle comes from your tongue," my genius man-child responded, "where does your voice come from?"

I loved it! I was winning at the stalling-for-time game! Although I am not a scientist, I gratefully knew that I could answer his sincere question.

"Your voice comes from your voice box, which is in your throat. When air blows across your voice box, a sound comes out! Isn't that amazing?"

Jordan looked out of his open window as he pondered my answer.

Just then, a little voice from the far back seat captured my attention.

"Mama," my four-year-old daughter Joy piped up, "if your whistle comes from your tongue and your voice comes from your throat, where does the song in your heart come from?"

With a sparkle in my eyes and a catch in my throat, as we turned into our driveway, I exclaimed, "Oh, Joy! The song in your heart comes from Jesus! Isn't that wonderful?"

Heart Inspection

What is your favorite hymn of the faith?

What is your favorite contemporary worship song?

What does it mean to "have a song in your heart"?

Heartfelt Prayer

Jesus, today I promise that I will sing to You all day long! I will sing of Your matchless love and of Your power! I will sing of Your mercies from morning until night! Thank You for placing a song in my heart. In Jesus's name, I pray. Amen.

Eternal Words

This is the day which the LORD has made; let's rejoice and be glad in it. —Psalm 118:24

Reading the Lyrics

Read Psalm 150.

DAY 31
Wired for Song

The choice to worship is perhaps the most powerful choice that a believer can make, especially during the difficult days of life. If you long to storm-proof your heart, you will choose to open your mouth and sing to your Creator even when you don't feel like it! Perhaps, the most vital time to choose to worship is *especially* when you don't feel like it!

Storms are assured this side of heaven's glory; you will not escape the hurricane of disappointment, the blizzard of pain, or the tornado of trauma as you live a life for the glory of God. Even Jesus said, *"In the world you have tribulation, but take courage; I have overcome the world"* (John 16:33).

If you deeply desire to keep your power at full strength during the storms of life, you will make the difficult but necessary decision to continue to sing loudly even in the rain. When I go through a storm in life, I may cry but I also will worship! I may sob but I also will sing! I may weep but I also will praise the Lord of my salvation. I have learned that the best time to praise the Lord is actually the very worst day of my life. Can you do that?

As Christians, we have a deep, spiritual joy that remains unhindered regardless of what is happening in the natural. The choice to worship in the storm is the determination to walk by faith and not by sight. The ability to rejoice while in intense human pain is actually a faith issue.

> *Consider it all joy, my brothers and sisters, when you encounter various trials, knowing that the testing of your faith produces endurance.*
> —James 1:2–3

The faith of a Christian who is able to rejoice in a trial grows stronger and even more durable than it was prior to the trial. The faith of a woman of God who is able to sing through her sorrow is more precious than the most valuable and durable commodity known to mankind! Are you that woman?

> *In this you greatly rejoice, even though now for a little while, if necessary, you have been distressed by various trials, so that the proof*

of your faith, being more precious than gold which perishes though tested by fire, may be found to result in praise, glory, and honor at the revelation of Jesus Christ. —1 Peter 1:6–7

We sing in the fires of life and during the storms of life because it is not our circumstances that we are worshipping. We are singing heartfelt praise to our good, good Father who is always working every detail of our lives for our good and for His glory. Do you believe that? Let me hear you sing!

Heart Inspection

Do you believe that it is possible to worship the Lord even when you don't like your life? Why or why not?

How is choosing to praise the Lord when you are going through a trial a faith issue?

Do you know someone who is going through a hard time? How can you encourage this friend today?

Heartfelt Prayer

Lord Jesus, I declare that I will sing in the rain! I have made the decision to worship You even when my heart is breaking. You are good and You are worthy of my highest praise. In Jesus's name, I pray. Amen.

Eternal Words

> Even if the fig tree does not blossom, and there is no fruit on the vines, if the yield of the olive fails, and the fields produce no food, even if the flock disappears from the fold, and there are no cattle in the stalls, yet I will triumph in the LORD, I will rejoice in the God of my salvation.   —Habakkuk 3:17–18

Reading the Lyrics
Read Psalm 95.

Greatly Rejoice!

Peter has always been my favorite disciple, perhaps because I can relate to his ardent and fierce personality.

Prior to Pentecost, Peter was fiery and impetuous; he was filled with emotions and opinions. Peter spoke first and thought later; he dozed and drooled rather than praying for Jesus in the garden of Gethsemane. Peter cut off the ear of a Roman soldier and then denied Christ three times. He failed his first test of faith when he only walked a few steps on the water before he went splashing under! I wonder if Peter dealt with failure issues, with self-esteem issues, and with comparison issues. Perhaps you have dealt with those same issues as Peter and I have.

Peter became a changed man after seeing the risen Lord and after being filled with the Holy Spirit at Pentecost. Those two experiences— recognizing Jesus as the risen Lord and then being filled with the power of the Spirit—will change any one of us from being a failure to being a faith-walker, just like it changed Peter.

Let's read some words that Peter wrote close to the end of his life:

And though you have not seen Him, you love Him, and though you do not see Him now, but believe in Him, you greatly rejoice with joy inexpressible and full of glory, obtaining as the outcome of your faith, the salvation of your souls. —1 Peter 1:8–9

Christianity does not focus on some abstract idea or an elusive fictional character; Christianity concentrates on one Person. Christianity makes no excuses for centralizing Jesus, the crucified Christ. We who follow Him by faith do not see Jesus now…although someday, we will! Until that grand day of completion, we are called to a life of faith, hope, and joy. We are challenged to *"greatly rejoice"* by Peter, the man who had laughed with Jesus, eaten with Jesus, journeyed with Jesus, and heard His teachings firsthand.

As disciples who have experienced Christ and have been filled with the power of the Holy Spirit, we can rejoice with an indescribable and glorious joy! When in doubt, we sing! When we are discouraged, we rejoice! When we are downcast, we break out into a worship song!

One of the most amazing aspects of this passage is that Peter was encouraging the persecuted church, which would face untold trauma and horror. His advice is as compelling today as it was two thousand years ago: we are a people who sing during the most difficult of human circumstances. It is both our calling and our identity.

Heart Inspection

Why do you believe that God allows His children to suffer? Note that I didn't say *causes* His children to suffer but *allows* it.

What is your default when life is hard? What is the first response to a painful situation?

Do you know anyone who is suffering today? Would you pray for this dear person and reach out to him or her in love?

Heartfelt Prayer

Jesus, help me to sing! Enable me to sing in the shower and to sing in the fire. I will choose to worship when I am driving and when I am waiting. I will rejoice because You are worthy of my highest praise. In Jesus's wonderful name, I pray. Amen.

Eternal Words

I will bless the LORD at all times; His praise shall continually be in my mouth. My soul will make its boast in the LORD; the humble will hear it and rejoice. Exalt the LORD with me, and let's exalt His name together.
—Psalm 34:1–3

Reading the Lyrics

Read 1 Peter 1:1–25.

DAY 33

The Great Exchange

Life is at once glorious and painful; it is simultaneously difficult and delightful. It is *oh, so easy* and even fulfilling to rejoice in the easy days of life...but what does one do when there are no flowers that line our pathway? Where is the song of the heart when the wilderness that is our habitat threatens to kill our joy? What do we do then?

Often, we are traumatized by all that is transpiring in our day-to-day happenings; it is at that precise moment of trauma when a spirit of heaviness rears its understandable but awful head. In the wake of crippling occurrences, we are often left with a weighty dirge in our spirits. If this is where you have found yourself today, the prophet Isaiah has a wise answer for you:

To appoint unto them that mourn in Zion, to give unto them beauty for ashes, the oil of joy for mourning, the garment of praise for the spirit of heaviness; that they might be called trees of righteousness, the planting of the Lord, *that he might be glorified.* —Isaiah 61:3 KJV

I have often referred to this passage of Scripture as *the great exchange.* When we choose to worship the Lord during a time of devastation, a miraculous transferal takes place—the Lord gives us His joy and takes away our grief. He removes the spirit of heaviness that has encompassed us and gives us a beautiful garment of praise.

If your life has been more painful and more discouraging than most, there is an appointment that is yours. You have been appointed by the Holy Spirit to sing a rare and precious hymn of praise in place of your mournful song. What an impressive assignment! Although you may *feel* like wailing, the Holy Spirit is offering you a much more dynamic option; He is inviting you into the presence of the Lord, where there is always fullness of joy! He is summoning you to meet with the One who designed you, to sing your song of thanksgiving to Him even when your heart is breaking. Will you do it?

The password into the presence of the Lord is a simple but sincere, "Thank You, God!" Choosing to worship even when you are being tormented by a relentless storm in life is the most powerful and pure choice you will ever make. You will find that singing in the storm becomes an umbrella of protection that is more glorious and fulfilling than any other melody of your life.

Heart Inspection

Think of a man or a woman in the Bible who went through a traumatic and difficult experience. How did this person react to the pain of their circumstances?

What is the most difficult experience you have ever gone through in life? How did you feel the Lord's presence during that time?

Are there lyrics to a song that have encouraged you when you were struggling?

Heartfelt Prayer

Lord Jesus, give me a song that soars over the wilderness and echoes through the valley of pain. I desire to sing more than I desire to wail. You are worthy of my highest praise and loudest song! In Jesus's name, I pray. Amen.

Eternal Words

But a time is coming, and even now has arrived, when the true worshipers will worship the Father in spirit and truth; for such people the Father seeks to be His worshipers. —John 4:23

Reading the Lyrics

Read Psalm 102.

A Song at Midnight

Would you travel to ancient Rome with me? Let's quietly but keenly observe the lives of Paul and Silas at a very dark moment and discover what they determined to do when life was cruel and unkind. (See Acts 16:22–30.)

Paul and Silas had been viciously and needlessly attacked by a mob of Roman citizens. Even the chief magistrates joined in the aggression, tearing off the robes of these two innocent, godly men while the crowd repeatedly and brutally assailed them. After the savage attack, Paul and Silas were unfairly thrown into a Roman prison cell.

Can you even imagine it? The ugly and painful bruises on their body were accompanied by open, bleeding wounds. The feet of these honorable men were fastened into stocks so that they would not be able to escape.

The smell of a Roman prison was horrifying; the odor of feces, urine, and vomit filled the cold cells with a stench that was pervasive. There were likely rats and other rodents that scampered around in the darkness, trying to feast on crumbs of stale, moldy bread.

It was midnight in this abhorrent place, the darkest time of the night. While other prisoners were groaning in pain or weeping with despair, Paul and Silas made an extraordinary choice. These two men who had been treated unfairly and who had been imprisoned without a trial, chose to lift their voices in a hymn of praise and worship their Savior. What an extraordinary decision! What amazing men!

When Paul and Silas made the willful determination to sing in the midnight hour, a miracle happened in that Roman prison cell. There was a massive earthquake, the prison doors flew open, and all of the prisoners' chains were instantly unfastened.

Your choice to worship the Lord in the middle of your pain will open miraculous doors in your life as well. When you sing in the dark, the chains that have held you in bondage will miraculously fall off.

One of the most powerful aspects of this biblical account is that as Paul and Silas choose to sing aloud, the other prisoners were listening to them. There is a world in bondage and in darkness that is listening for the song of *your* life as well. Will you sing with Paul and Silas?

Heart Inspection
What chains in your life need to be broken?

_____

_____

Why is it important to sing at the midnight hour in life?

_____

_____

Besides Jesus, who is your favorite New Testament character and why?

_____

_____

Heartfelt Prayer

Oh, Jesus! How I love singing my song of praise to You! Thank You for opening miraculous doors in my life and for breaking chains that have held me in bondage. I will sing a glorious song for the world to hear! In Jesus's name, I pray. Amen.

Eternal Words

The Lord is my strength and song, and He has become my salvation; this is my God, and I will praise Him; my father's God, and I will exalt Him. —Exodus 15:2

Reading the Lyrics
Read Acts 16:22–40.

My Midnight Hour

Cancer had filled both of my breasts. The doctors felt that my only option was to have a double mastectomy, followed by months of vile but necessary treatment. My heart was brave but I knew that my body would be forever changed.

My husband and daughter prayed for me and then watched me being wheeled through the ominous hospital doors for surgery. I turned my head to smile at them and saw some of the people who I loved the most in the entire world: my husband, my daughter, her best friend, and my dear college roommate who had come to take care of me.

The hours following the traumatic surgery are a blur of pain and discomfort. My four companions were gathered around my bed and prayed for me as I fought my way into consciousness. All I could say to them was, "Sing to me!"

And so they sang.

"Great Is Thy Faithfulness" turned to "I'd Rather Have Jesus" and then "How Great Is Our God." Whenever the voices of the quartet began to fade away, I quickly but quietly demanded, "Sing over me!" And so the a cappella serenade continued with "Oh, How I Love Jesus," "Turn Your Eyes Upon Jesus," and "In the Presence of Jehovah."

The minutes turned into hours and yet all I could do was to beg them to sing in my sterile hospital room. "Amazing Grace," "What a Friend We Have in Jesus," and "It is No Secret (What God Can Do)" filled the silence of the night.

Finally, about midnight, my dear husband Craig said to me, "Honey, the girls need to go home. It's late. Debby and I need to rest. Would it be all right if we stop singing now?"

I opened my bloodshot eyes and stubbornly said, "That's fine. You can stop singing, but call Kelly on the phone. She will sing over me even if you won't!" Kelly was our dear worship leader and is truly like another daughter to me.

So, Craig took out his cell phone at midnight, woke Kelly up from a deep sleep, and asked her to sing over me. And she did! She sang for hours, and my soul was at rest. The Lord's presence filled that place of undeserved pain and loneliness. He was with me! What a gift!

Heart Inspection

When you are weary or in pain, who would you call to sing over your life?

_____

_____

Why is it necessary for a believer in Jesus Christ to sing at the midnight hour?

_____

_____

What is the difference between praise and worship?

_____

_____

Heartfelt Prayer

Lord, I am determined to sing in pain and to sing in the dark. I promise to sing when I am healthy and to sing when I am sick. Jesus, I confess today that nothing—absolutely nothing—will mute the song of my heart. I declare that I will always sing Your praises. In Jesus's name, I pray. Amen.

Eternal Words

Through Him then, let's continually offer up a sacrifice of praise to God, that is, the fruit of lips praising His name. —Hebrews 13:15

Reading the Lyrics

Read Ephesians 1:2–12.

Part Six:
Building Materials –
The Fruit of the Spirit

Fruit is always the miraculous, the created; it is never the result of willing, but always a growth. The fruit of the Spirit is a gift of God, and only He can produce it. They who bear it know as little about it as the tree knows of its fruit. They know only the power of Him on whom their life depends.

—Dietrich Bonhoeffer

Your life is not your own, and your heart was never meant to be a place of bitterness, discontent, or gloom. The Father created the heart that you call home to be a place where His presence is unmeasured and where the personality of the Holy Spirit is alive and dynamic. It's time to serve up an abundant portion of the fruits of the Holy Spirit from the storehouse of your heart.

DAY 36

The Fabric of Home

But the fruit of the Spirit is love, joy, peace, patience, kindness, goodness, faithfulness, gentleness, self-control; against such things there is no law.
—Galatians 5:22–23

Recently, my husband and I were on the hunt for a new home. We had been living in a rental property for two years and couldn't wait to own our own home again. We were thrilled to be able to purchase a home in which we could entertain and celebrate holidays. We were nearly giddy with excitement to vacate the second-rate rental house and then place our roots deeply and lovingly into a home that was ours—all ours!

We looked at every home in the area that was in our price range, and nothing seemed to suffice. Some homes were big enough, but they were the consummate fixer-uppers—and Craig didn't want that! Other homes were in top-notch condition, but were lacking a yard, or a place for our grand piano, or a suitable kitchen.

Our sweet realtor finally convinced us to consider buying a new home rather than an older one. We were enthralled by the process and quickly made an offer on a home that only had the foundation laid and the framework completed. I couldn't believe it! I would be living in a brand new home that no one else had ever occupied! I would have the delight of selecting the countertops, the paint colors, the flooring, and the light fixtures!

When the day finally came for me to meet with the design team, I thought that my heart would literally escape from the confines of my chest. I couldn't control the adrenaline or the anticipation. Oh, my, was it ever overwhelming! And yet I loved every single minute of it! I knew that the colors, the materials, the lighting fixtures, the flooring, the cabinetry, and even the smallest details like the wall switch plates would set the tone of our home for years to come.

So it is with your heart, my friend. It matters what building materials comprise the sustenance and the fabric of your heart, so choose well. It's time for you to choose the building materials of the heart that you call home.

As you intentionally determine what habits, attitudes, and atmosphere will adorn your heart, I'd like to suggest that you consider the fruits of the Holy Spirit. These fruits will make your heart a place of vibrant living, unmatched ministry, and sincere friendship. As you choose these specific personality traits that the Holy Spirit offers to anyone who chooses to cultivate them, you will discover that your heart holds a breathtaking similarity to the heart of your King.

Heart Inspection

What three words would you currently use to describe yourself? Be honest!

_____

_____

What three words do you think that a friend would use to describe you? You might even want to ask a dear friend this question in order to receive an honest answer.

_____

_____

What three words would you love people to use in their description of you?

_____

_____

Heartfelt Prayer

Jesus, help me grow to be more like You every day. I long for the content of my heart to reflect the love, joy, and peace that belong to You. I deeply desire for my character to match Yours. In Jesus's name, I pray. Amen.

Eternal Words

Remain in Me, and I in you. Just as the branch cannot bear fruit of itself but must remain in the vine, so neither can you unless you remain in Me. I am the vine, you are the branches; the one who remains in Me, and I in him bears much fruit, for apart from Me you can do nothing. —John 15:4–5

Feasting on the Word

Read Galatians 5.

DAY 37

The Greatest of All

*But the fruit of the Spirit is **love**…*
—Galatians 5:22

Songs have been written about it, books have expounded upon it, poets have built legacies because of it, and holidays are focused on its devoted nature.

Is it really love that makes the world go 'round? Is it also true that "all you need is love"? I can assure you that true love is so much more than a song, more eternal than a chapter, greater than a verse, and exponentially more dynamic than a single day of the calendar year.

Love is not some adolescent ideal, nor is it a weak acceptance of a person's compromising behavior. Love believes for the absolute best and seeks the highest dignity in a person's life. True love is a deep compassion that invites a sinner out of sin and into relationship with Him whose very name and nature is Love.

Love is active and never passive. Love loudly speaks words of encouragement and perpetually sings songs of tender understanding. Love is not afraid to confront sin with the truth, and it stands firmly upon the principles of God. True love is not insipid, neither is it anemic or lacking in character; unconditional love will always fight for upright behavior and heartfelt integrity.

You probably know that *agape*, the Greek word for "love," is used in the list of the fruits of the Holy Spirit. *Agape* love communicates a benevolence that cannot be conquered; nothing can defeat this type of love. This invincible love means that no matter how someone speaks or acts toward us, we will never seek anything but the highest virtue for that person. My! That's difficult, isn't it?

True love can be described as a commitment to a deliberate effort of bringing out the highest good in a person. But *the highest good* does not mean acceptance of sin or compromising behavior. As a believer in Christ, we know that any good in us is a reflection of Christ and His gospel; therefore, as those who are called to love, we must fight for what is right in a person and be brave enough to confront the compromise. My! That's difficult, too, isn't it?

So, what is love? How can I build a life upon the love that the Bible promotes? Only as I know Jesus and become more like Him am I able to love sinners and friends. Only as I read His story am I able to write an unforgettable love story with my life. Only as I worship Him am I able to sing a love song that will never be silenced. If love is to be the strongest fabric of my life, then I must choose to love like Jesus does.

Heart Inspection

Who has been the most difficult person for you to love in your life?

_____

_____

What can you do to encourage that difficult person this week?

_____

_____

What is your definition of the word "love"?

_____

_____

Heartfelt Prayer

Jesus, I want to be just like You. I want to love difficult people and to have compassion for those who are cruel. Lord, would You love others through me? In Jesus's name, I pray. Amen.

Eternal Words

Beloved, let's love one another; for love is from God, and everyone who loves has been born of God and knows God. The one who does not love does not know God, because God is love. —1 John 4:7–8

Feasting on the Word

Read 1 Corinthians 13.

The Joy of Joy!

But the fruit of the Spirit is love, **joy…**
—Galatians 5:22

In fifth grade, my beloved teacher, Miss Sullivan, taught her curious class of eleven-year-olds that in order to define a certain word, one should never use the word itself in the definition. The rule that Miss Sullivan taught all of her eager students is an accepted grammatical rule that most savvy writers and wordsmiths follow implicitly.

However, I have discovered that it is nearly impossible to define the word "joy" without using the word itself in the definition.

The Hebrew definition of the word *simchah* is "joy, mirth, gladness; the joy of God."

The Greek definition of the word *chara* is "joy, gladness; the cause of occasion of one's joy."

Due to my frustration as a grammar elitist who is convinced that substance is lacking when using a word in its own definition, I decided to dig a bit deeper and to valiantly endeavor to discover the root definition of the word "joy."

"Joy wrought by the Holy Spirit" was a definition that resonated a bit stronger in my frustrated soul because at least it gave some credit to the Holy Spirit.

And then, at last, I came upon this definition from a Hebrew dictionary I found among my grandfather's archaic library: *"The blessedness that the Lord enjoys around the throne of God Himself."*

Wow! What a heart-stopping definition of this glorious word that is so profoundly difficult to define! I must share it with you again so that you can linger on it with me: *"The blessedness that the Lord enjoys around the throne of God Himself."*

Although this particular definition does indeed use a derivative of the word "joy" in the word "enjoys," I found myself completely agreeing with this ancient meaning found among stacks of dusty, dog-eared books.

Joy is the atmosphere of heaven! Joy is the very air that God the Father Himself breathes every day of eternity. And, wonder of wonders, because joy is heaven's delivered gift to me while I walk on planet Earth, it is my delight and strength to experience the blessedness that God on His throne enjoys. While I am living in time, I am the beneficiary of eternal joy.

Joy is God's indescribable gift to us as we contently snuggle into His presence and hunker down into all that He is and all that He gives.

Heart Inspection

How does "joy" differ from "happiness"?

_____

_____

What was the most joyful moment of your life?

_____

_____

Is it possible to "choose joy"?

_____

_____

Heartfelt Prayer

Loving Jesus, would You make my life a showcase of Your joy? Would You use my broken, dilapidated life as a trophy of heaven's joy? I give myself to You anew today and I ask You to fill every corner of my heart with Your indescribable joy! In Jesus's name, I pray. Amen.

Eternal Words

You will make known to me the way of life; in Your presence is fullness of joy; in Your right hand there are pleasures forever.
—Psalm 16:11

Feasting on the Word

Read Psalm 51:10–13; Nehemiah 8:10; 1 Peter 1:6–9.

It Surpasses All Understanding

*But the fruit of the Spirit is love, joy, **peace**...*
—Galatians 5:22

How wonderful to know that we, as believers in Jesus Christ, can experience victorious peace in the middle of the fierce storms of life!

How wonderful to know that we, as believers in Jesus Christ, have a wise peace that trumps even our own understanding!

How wonderful to know that we, as believers in Jesus Christ, have a tenacious peace even in the middle of conflict.

How wonderful to know!

Peace is the magnificent legacy that has been given to us by Jesus Christ as we live in a world of pain, compromise, and sin.

Peace I leave you, My peace I give you; not as the world gives, do I give to you. Do not let your hearts be troubled, nor fearful.
—John 14:27

The peace that is yours in Christ is not attached to your circumstances, nor is it a byproduct of your human relationships. Your astonishing peace is extracted from the goodness and the authority of God. You can live with a miraculous peace in your heart and in your mind because you know that the promises of God are true! Peace is the ruling attitude in your soul because you are assured that He is working all things together for good! You can bask in the peace of the Father because you have faith that He will certainly accomplish what concerns you.

Fear is not able to steal your peace, nor is conflict able to erase your peace. Peace is not an earthly response to one's circumstances, but it is a rare gift bestowed upon those who choose to trust fully in the character of God.

The steadfast of mind You will keep in perfect peace, because he trusts in You.
                                              —Isaiah 26:3

I have learned that it is futile to pray for peace while my mind is embracing anxiety. I must set aside worry and choose to simply trust the Lord and all of His ways. When I trust the One who made me, the One who saved me, the One who forgave me, and the One who loves me unconditionally, it is in that moment that peace floods my soul and worry exits my heart. Trust always begets peace.

You were created to live a life of peace and rest, even during the difficult days of life. There is only one way to find peace when your world is falling apart, and that is by falling on your knees and declaring, "Lord, I trust You and all of Your ways!"

Heart Inspection

What is your definition of the word "peace"?

Who is the most peaceful person you know? What do you believe to be the source of their peace?

What are you most worried about today? Can you trust God with that situation?

Heartfelt Prayer

Lord Jesus, I confess that I trust You today. I trust in Your goodness and in Your power. I trust Your authority and Your wisdom. I trust in Your promises and in Your plan. In Jesus's name, I pray. Amen.

Eternal Word

The LORD will give strength to His people; the LORD will bless His people with peace.   —Psalm 29:11

Feasting on the Word

Read Romans 8.

The Family Business

*But the fruit of the Spirit is love, joy, peace, **patience**…*
—Galatians 5:22

Oh, to exhibit the patience of God in my life! Oh, to have the unsurpassed ability to suffer long through others' insults, betrayal, and cool indifference toward me. Oh, to bear with those who refuse to bear with me!

I have always thought it so interesting that the word "patience" is often translated as the compound word "long-suffering." Patience is a virtue toward which I can strive, but long-suffering? I am not sure about that one!

Honestly, I don't suffer well in the short-term situations in life, so being challenged by the Holy Spirit to "suffer long" seems to be too massive of a challenge.

The Greek word *makrothymise* can be translated as "patience" or "forbearance" as well as "long-suffering." Interestingly, it is the word that is most commonly used in the New Testament to describe the heart of God and Jesus toward you and me.

Or do you think lightly of the riches of His kindness and restraint and patience, not knowing that the kindness of God leads you to repentance? —Romans 2:4

There was an esteemed church father and preacher by the name of John Chrysostom who said of *makrothymise*, "It is the grace of the man who could revenge himself and who does not."

If the Father had the same heart that we demonstrate, the heart of mankind, He would have destroyed this world centuries ago. However, our God displays *makrothymise* toward us and refuses to obliterate His creation. Rather, He pursues us with His love and with His kindness. As the daughter of the King, I must be about the family business and engage in the production of *makrothymise* toward those in my world. I must—I simply must!—be a vessel of the patience, kindness, forbearance, compassion, and forgiveness of my Father.

Patience is not only a matter of being slow to anger, but it also has a dynamic, proactive meaning as well. *Makrothymise* also carries the meaning of bearing one up or carrying another. Ours is a family business of bearing one another's burdens and making another's load lighter. We encourage those who are weak and pray for those in pain. We serve those who are sick and we love those who struggle. It is, after all, what Dad would do.

Heart Inspection

What is your definition of the word "patience"?

_____

_____

Who is it difficult for you to be patient with?

_____

_____

How did today's devotional help your heart attitude toward those with whom you have been impatient?

_____

_____

Heartfelt Prayer

Jesus, I want to be just like You! Give me the muscle of patience and of forbearance. I pray that You would bring people in my life who need more of You. In Your name, I pray. Amen.

Eternal Words

Love is patient, love is kind, it is not jealous; love does not brag, it is not arrogant. It does not act disgracefully, it does not seek its own benefit; it is not provoked, does not keep an account of a wrong suffered.
—1 Corinthians 13:4–5

Feasting on the Word

Read Colossians 3.

Not the Same, But Together

But the fruit of the Spirit is love, joy, peace,
*patience, **kindness, goodness**...*
—Galatians 5:22

At first glance, one might think that kindness and goodness are inter-changeable, but that is not the case. Kindness and goodness, although closely connected, have their own personalities and possess a unique pur-pose in our hearts.

The Greek word for kindness is *chrestotes,* which is also used in the New Testament to describe the yoke of Christ. (See Matthew 11:30.) The yoke of Christ is gentle in that it fits well or does not chafe. *Chrestotes* can also be translated as being mellow or sweet, much like old wine. Jesus exhibited *cherstotes* when He was kind to the sinning woman who had anointed His feet.

A truly kind person makes the lives of others sweeter and easier simply by their gracious presence. Kindness is an aroma of the heart that is at once both sweet and purposeful. There is no such thing as a small act of kindness for every act of kindness leaves perpetual ripples in the sea of life. Kindness costs no money yet it is an attribute of eternal value. Kindness turns an ordinary human being into a hero and gives a common man or woman a rich legacy.

The Greek word *agathosune* is a strictly biblical term that was never used in secular Greek society. Theologians have described this word as "a goodness that makes one good for something," or "an uprightness of heart and life, goodness, kindness." Jesus expressed *agathosune* when He chased the money changers out of the temple. The goodness of Jesus demanded a change and required a response. Living a life of innate goodness demands a struggle against not only evil, but also against the culture and against temptation. Goodness might be the most costly of the fruits of the Spirit because it demands the exacting price of self-discipline and the courage to stand up against evil.

Henry David Thoreau was once jailed because he refused to pay a poll tax to a state that supported slavery. His dear friend, Ralph Waldo Emerson, paid a visit to him in the putrid conditions of jail and worriedly asked, "What are you doing in jail, Henry?"

Thoreau's response has caused me great self-examination over the years. He told Emerson, "Nay, Ralph. The question is, 'What are you doing out there?'"

Heart Inspection

How do goodness and kindness differ?

_____

_____

Is there any similarity between kindness and goodness?

_____

_____

Of these two character traits, which do you need to cultivate to a greater degree in yourself?

_____

_____

Heartfelt Prayer

> Heavenly Father, I want everything that You have for me. I want to be kind like Christ was kind and I want to go about doing good just like He did. Give me the strength for both. In Jesus's name, I pray. Amen.

Eternal Words

> *Do not let kindness and truth leave you; bind them around your neck, write them on the tablet of your heart.*   —Proverbs 3:3

Feasting on the Word

Read Luke 7:36–50.

The Powerful Trio

But the fruit of the Spirit is love, joy, peace, patience, kindness, goodness,
faithfulness, gentleness, self-control*; against such things there is no law.*
—Galatians 5:22–23

Are you reliable? Are you considerate? Have you mastered the desires of the flesh?

As I attempt to answer these invasive questions, I realize how much I am in desperate need of all that God is and, unfortunately, how much flesh has reared its ugly head in me. Today we will linger over the final three building materials that the Holy Spirit is offering as we seek to establish a heart that is fit for our King.

Faithfulness is the Greek word *pistis* and it simply means being reliable, especially in the matters of our faith. I can be faithful because I serve a God who is faithful. But the wonder of it all is that even when I am faithless, He is faithful still!

If we are faithless, He remains faithful, for He cannot deny Himself.
—2 Timothy 2:13

Most Bible scholars agree that "gentleness" or *praotes* is the most untranslatable of the words in this descriptive list. *Praotes* can mean being submissive to the will of God, or it can mean being teachable. However, the closest modern translation to this ancient word is "being considerate." The great teacher Aristotle defined *praotes* as "the mean between excessive anger and excessive angerlessness; the quality of the man who is always angry at the right time and never at the wrong time." Gentleness is often translated as meekness. As you consider the building materials of your heart, I hope that you will choose the strength of meekness.

And finally, we come to the fruit that we all presume will taste bitter… yet that is not true at all. Self-control is the mastery of one's self, and it will never happen in your life without the power of the Holy Spirit. An athlete knows the benefits of self-control, and we must align our hearts and minds with the athleticism of a spiritual champion. We must recognize those things that are beneficial to our walk in Christ and refuse those habits or attitudes that give freedom to impulse or desire. Self-control enables us to prepare our lives for service in the kingdom of God. It should never be a dreaded, religious practice, but should always open the door of joy!

Heart Inspection

After reading today's lesson, how would you define faithfulness?

_____

_____

How would you define gentleness?

_____

_____

How would you define self-control?

_____

_____

Heartfelt Prayer

Jesus, would You inspect my heart today? Would You point out those areas in my life that need improvement? Would You help me to reflect Your character and Your nature? In Jesus's name, I pray. Amen.

Eternal Words

Search me, God, and know my heart; put me to the test and know my anxious thoughts; and see if there is any hurtful way in me, and lead me in the everlasting way. —Psalm 139:23–24

Feasting on the Word

Read Jeremiah 17:5–10.

Part Seven: Housekeeping – Forgiveness

To be a Christian means to forgive the inexcusable because God has forgiven the inexcusable in you.
—C. S. Lewis

Every home experiences clutter from time to time, and your heart is no different. This week, we will take out the cleaning products provided by the Lord and then clean our hearts, ensuring that they are free from any envy, bitterness, and shame. By the end of this week, your heart will be a sparkling demonstration of the power of forgiveness!

A Sparkling Clean Heart

I absolutely love a sparkling clean home, don't you? Now, I am quick to admit that I despise the *process* of cleaning my home, but I adore the *result* that it provides! I would so much rather read a good book than force myself to dust under my bed. I would completely choose to go for a much-anticipated walk in God's creation rather than unload that dreaded dishwasher. I find unmatched delight in talking to one of my children on the phone, but dusting? Vacuuming? Doing the laundry? No! Not my cup of tea!

However, I do love the smell of a clean home, the satisfaction of an uncluttered space, and the sparkle of dust-free furniture. My dilemma is that I just don't want to be involved in the process required to procure the results!

Heart-cleaning is much like housework. One must understand the value of an uncluttered, sparkling clean heart in order to appreciate the process. You really don't want a heart that is filled with yesterday's baggage, with gross, putrid bitterness, or with trash bags filled with unforgiveness, do you? An orderly, fresh heart is the finest place to live one's life. So let's get to it!

Forgiveness is the serious business of Christianity; it is not to be ignored or presumed to be unimportant. Grace is not cheap, and you must always bear in mind that Jesus paid an enormously high price for you, which, in turn, requires you to forgive everyone all the time! Forgiveness is one of the most important tenets of Christianity; forgiveness demands that we, as His children, absolutely refuse to hold grudges against others who are made in the image of God.

Trust, however, is a different process altogether. Forgiveness always precedes trust, but trust is not always a necessity. You can forgive someone without then trusting their behavior or choices.

We are not a bitter people, and we certainly should never look for the opportunity for revenge. Christians should always choose to forgive and even anticipate opportunities to bless those who have wronged them. We obey God, we forgive, we bless those who have hurt us, and we pray for our enemies! It is just how we do life, and it is part of the process of housecleaning our hearts.

When you choose to rid your heart of yesterday's bitterness, you will love the results. When you decide that it is time to forgive someone who has mistreated you, your heart will be a sparkling representation of the glory of God. When you give grace to someone who has rejected you or even betrayed you, you will be amazed at the sweet aroma that surrounds the atmosphere of your heart.

Heart Inspection

Do you feel that residual bitterness is cluttering your heart?

Who do you need to forgive?

Write out a brief definition of the word "forgiveness."

Heartfelt Prayer

Jesus, I am ready. I am ready to clean out the corners of my heart. I am ready to forgive others just as You have forgiven me. Thank You, Father, for Your grace. In Jesus's name, I pray. Amen.

Eternal Words

In Him we have redemption through His blood, the forgiveness of our wrongdoings, according to the riches of His grace. —Ephesians 1:7

Cleaning Supplies

Read Ephesians 1.

What Would Jesus Do?

The most beloved prayer that has ever been uttered is found in Matthew 6 and Luke 11. This well-known prayer is simply known as the Lord's Prayer. Let's linger over these words spoken by Jesus to His disciples after one of them said to Him, *"Lord, teach us to pray"* (Luke 11:1).

> *Our Father, who is in heaven, hallowed be Your name. Your kingdom come. Your will be done, on earth as it is in heaven. Give us this day our daily bread. And forgive us our debts, as we also have forgiven our debtors. And do not lead us into temptation, but deliver us from evil.* —Matthew 6:9–13

Some faith traditions also add what is known as the doxology: "For the kingdom and the power and the glory are Yours, now and forever. Amen."

The Lord's Prayer has stood the test of time for over two millennia. Songs have been written based upon this prayer, and sermons have been preached based upon its content. It is the most familiar of all spoken prayers throughout all of written history. However, sometimes in its familiarity, I fear that we have lost its deep and compelling meaning.

When this prayer is closely examined, there is a key to it that is enveloped in the middle of the verbiage. *"Forgive us our debts, as we also have forgiven our debtors."* I believe that forgiveness is not optional, but mandatory for those who have danced in the freedom of Christ. Forgiveness is central to our prayer lives; if we pray, we must forgive.

After Jesus gave the disciples the model of how to pray, He added a stirring addendum to the teaching moment. Jesus wasn't content to allow this prayer to end at "amen," but He chose to repeat this aspect of forgiveness. Let's read on:

> *For if you forgive other people for their offenses, your heavenly Father will also forgive you. But if you do not forgive other people, then your Father will not forgive your offenses.* —Matthew 6:14–15

The single point that Jesus reiterated outside of the context of the exact prayer is the importance of forgiveness. When Jesus bids His followers to specific behavior twice in the same conversation, I believe that we must obey immediately and without question.

When my children were young, I would often remind them, "Delayed obedience is disobedience." Perhaps today would be an appropriate moment to immediately obey the Lord's command to forgive others.

Heart Inspection

Why do you believe that Jesus repeated His instructions to forgive others in this conversation? Why wasn't once enough?

_____

_____

Reread Matthew 6:14–15. Can you put this verse into your own words?

_____

_____

Why is forgiveness such an important part of the heart cleaning that we are currently doing?

_____

_____

Heartfelt Prayer

Jesus, thank You for Your forgiveness. Thank You for dying on the cross and for forgiving my sins. I am a sinner and You are my Savior. I receive Your forgiveness today in Your name. Amen.

Eternal Words

But You are a God of forgiveness, gracious and compassionate, slow to anger and abounding in mercy. —Nehemiah 9:17

Cleaning Supplies

Read Psalm 130.

Forgiveness and Prayer

Yesterday's devotional was a stirring reminder of the priority that Jesus has placed on forgiveness. Let's take the time to reread the admonition that Jesus gave to the disciples right after He taught them to pray the Lord's Prayer:

> *For if you forgive other people for their offenses, your heavenly Father will also forgive you. But if you do not forgive other people, then your Father will not forgive your offenses.* —Matthew 6:14–15

Knowing that Jesus spoke these words immediately after He taught the disciples how to pray, is it possible that prayers may go unanswered and are not as powerful as they could potentially be when prayed with unforgiveness in our hearts?

Based on the words of Jesus, can you consider the possibility that prayer will not yield the results you desire if you are holding bitterness or anger in your heart toward a sister or a brother in the Lord?

These verses in the Gospel of Matthew clearly state a fact that we cannot ignore: there is a correlation between our forgiveness of others and the Father's ability to forgive us. I can assure you completely that these verses are not referring to salvation but to forgiveness. These are verses of discipline in a Christian's life, and this tenet of Christianity must be embraced.

If you sow forgiveness to others, then you will reap forgiveness from your Father. The profound kingdom principle is this: *"What you plant will always be the very thing you harvest"* (Galatians 6:7 TPT). If you sow mercy, you will reap mercy; if you sow judgment, you will reap judgment. (See Matthew 5:7; 7:1.)

Often, we may think of this principle only in terms of sowing our tithe and offerings, and then reaping a harvest with a pay raise or bonus at work, or even winning the lottery. This principle, however, does not only apply to our finances, but it rings true in every attitude sown, in every hour spent in prayer, and in every fruit of the Spirit that we share with others. You will unconditionally and absolutely reap what you sow in life this side of heaven.

Whenever you stand praying, forgive, if you have anything against anyone, so that your Father who is in heaven will also forgive you for your offenses. But if you do not forgive, neither will your Father who is in heaven forgive your offenses. —Mark 11:25–26

Every day is an appropriate day to ask the Father to show you if you have unforgiveness hiding in the corners of your heart. There is no room for bitterness in the heart of a believer in Christ. We are a people who have been gloriously forgiven and, as such, we can do no less than to forgive others who have also been made in the image of God, our loving Father.

Heart Inspection

Do you believe that there is a correlation between forgiveness and prayer? Why or why not?

_____

_____

Why is forgiveness of premier importance in your walk with Christ?

_____

_____

Heartfelt Prayer

Jesus, I ask today that You give me the power and the desire to forgive those who have betrayed me or even abused me. I refuse to hold onto the pain of my past, but I forgive willingly and freely. In Jesus's name, I pray. Amen.

Eternal Words

And if he sins against you seven times a day, and returns to you seven times, saying, "I repent," you shall forgive him. —Luke 17:4

Cleaning Supplies

Read Matthew 18:21–35.

When You Made the Mess

It has been my experience that the hardest person for me to forgive is…me. I can easily forgive my children or my friends, but when it is necessary to forgive myself, I just can't do it. I can easily forgive my husband, politicians, and that driver who cut me off in traffic. However, I have been known to dig my feet into the ground, cross my arms, and stubbornly refuse to forgive myself when I have done something that I should not have done.

There have been times when I have beat myself into an emotional pulp after making a glaring mistake, and then I have climbed into a hidden place where no one could reach me. I have thrown pity party after pity party on my behalf and have convinced myself that God could never use someone with my numerous faults.

When I have made a mess in life, I must clean it up. And it often all begins by humbly forgiving myself. Just as I offer unconditional grace to others, I must also offer it to myself. Just as I walk in compassion and tender mercies with others, I can do no less for me—a woman who God loves dearly and who has been made in His very image.

Corrie ten Boom, one of my heroines of the faith, once said that when God forgives one of His children, He buries their sins in the deepest part of the sea and puts up a "No Fishing Allowed" sign in that place! If God has forgiven you and has buried your sins, you must follow His gracious example.

When a sin from your past tries to remind you of your failures, remind yourself of God's goodness and forbearance in your life. When you feel unworthy and wonder if you are good enough to be used by God, remind yourself of these great men and women of the faith:

+ Moses killed a man.
+ Sarah lied and was impatient with God's plan in her life.
+ David stole another man's wife.
+ Jonah ran from God in disobedience.
+ Peter cut off a man's ear and denied Christ three times.
+ Paul assassinated Christians.
+ Mary Magdalene once harbored seven demons.

Just as you have forgiven others, today is the day to forgive yourself! Walk ahead in confidence and boldness, knowing that the only type of people God uses is imperfect people! You are in good company even with your weaknesses and failures. If God says that you are forgiven and that He can use you, don't argue with God!

Heart Inspection

Imagine a list of all of your misdeeds being published on social media. What would your response be?

_____

_____

Now, how does it feel not just to be forgiven for your sins, but also to have them all put *out of sight* by God?

_____

_____

Heartfelt Prayer

Jesus, today I forgive myself. I forgive myself for causing pain in other people's lives and I forgive myself for not living the way that You have called me to live. Give me the power and the desire to live for You! In Jesus's name, I pray. Amen.

Eternal Words

Blessed are those whose lawless deeds have been forgiven, and whose sins have been covered.   —Romans 4:7

Cleaning Supplies

Read 1 John 1.

The Hallway of Your Heart

I have found that when I have a difficult time forgiving someone in my life, it is an indication that there is likely a schism in my relationship with God. If I am unable to forgive a friend, family member, or acquaintance who is made in the very image of God, then it is time for some examination of my relationship with Father God.

When I find it formidable to forgive someone, I often pray this Scripture over my own life:

Search me, God, and know my heart; put me to the test and know my anxious thoughts; and see if there is any hurtful way in me, and lead me in the everlasting way. —Psalm 139:23–24

If I am unable to forgive others, I must thoroughly probe the hallway in my heart that leads to the throne room of God. Have I allowed sinful dust and discarded habits to clutter my prayer life? Have I welcomed worry and anxiety into my thought life and therefore replaced the vitality of trust?

If I am unable to forgive someone, myself included, I am rebelling against God and all that He stands for. I am standing in direct opposition to the One who created me, who loves me unconditionally, and who gives me the breath of life every single day.

When I am struggling with forgiveness, these are some questions that I must ask myself:

+ When was the last time that I read my Bible?
+ When was the last time that I uttered a prayer of deep thanksgiving?
+ When was the last time that I broke out into a song of joyful worship?
+ When was the last time that I fasted?
+ When was the last time that I spent time on my knees in prayer?

God's ways are infinitely higher than our ways; forgiveness is always taking the high road with God and to God. If you long to live above your human pain, you will run to the Father in utter abandonment, and you will allow Him to search your human heart. You will submit your preferences, opinions, and offenses to His higher grace.

And, you will say with Jesus, *"Father, forgive them; for they do not know what they are doing"* (Luke 23:34).

Heart Inspection

How close do you feel to God today?

_____

_____

If you feel far away, what can you do to draw closer?

_____

_____

If you feel close to Him, why is that? What have you done to draw close?

_____

_____

Heartfelt Prayer

Jesus, I want more of You! I want to live my very life in Your wonderful presence! I thank You that when I draw close to You, You draw close to me! In Jesus's name, I pray. Amen.

Eternal Words

Submit therefore to God. But resist the devil, and he will flee from you. Come close to God and He will come close to you.

—James 4:7–8

Cleaning Supplies

Read Romans 8:1–25.

Decorate with Grace

"Grace" is such a lovely word, isn't it? When you know the meaning behind this sweet yet formidable word, you will hang grace in every room of your heart! When you understand the unmatched potency that grace holds, you will display it for the world to see.

I have a dear friend, Carolyn, who lives in one of the most beautiful homes I have ever had the pleasure to visit. Carolyn is the consummate southern hostess and I have spent many long hours curled up with a book on her front porch underneath the low-hanging ceiling fans, praying with tears running down my cheeks in her sunroom, and sitting at her kitchen table enjoying delicious food and refreshing conversation!

In every room of Carolyn's pleasant and winsome home, if you look closely, you will discover that there is a cross hanging on a wall, a cross painted in a picture, or a cross simply lying on an end table. Carolyn's goal is to have a meaningful cross in every room of her house just so that she is reminded often of the price that Jesus paid for her sins.

Carolyn also says that the visual demonstration of displaying a cross in every room reminds her to forgive others when they have wronged her. Carolyn sincerely says, "I just can't escape the grace of the cross of Christ!"

Have you tried to escape grace? Have you hidden it away for no one to see? Or is it on glorious and obvious display in your miraculous life?

Grace includes forgiveness, repentance, regeneration, and salvation. In short, grace is the whole of God's activity toward mankind.

But He gives a greater grace.   —James 4:6

Would you reread those six wonder-filled words and just allow the meaning of them to fill your soul with amazement?

"But He gives a greater grace."

"Grace" is the unmerited favor of God! You did nothing to deserve it, nothing to earn it. And you will do nothing to keep it. God gives His grace freely and it empowers us to live for Him. The first taste of grace is offered at salvation when we are forgiven for our sins. However, grace doesn't stop there! Grace continues on and on and manifests itself in every room of our heart.

Grace gives us hope when our prayers have turned desperate; grace is the strength that we need in times of weakness.

Grace gives us focus to face yet another battle; grace stirs up God's love within our hearts for others. Grace reminds us to run to the promises of God and it is wrapped up in the peace that surpasses understanding.

We need God's grace to forgive, to live, to endure, and to sing. I hope that you will hang the grace of God in every room of your heart!

Heart Inspection

What emotions come to the surface of your heart as you read the verse, *"But He gives a greater grace"*?

_____

_____

How have you experienced the grace of God in your life?

_____

_____

How have you offered the grace of God to others?

_____

_____

Heartfelt Prayer

Jesus, I long for grace to be on display in my life! Use me as a conduit for Your miraculous grace in the lives of others. In Jesus's name, I pray. Amen.

Eternal Words

For the LORD God is a sun and shield; the LORD gives grace and glory; He withholds no good thing from those who walk with integrity. —Psalm 84:11

Cleaning Supplies

Read Zechariah 4:6–10.

A Sacred Summons

You and I have been invited by Jesus Christ to be His disciples. Just as Jesus looked into the faces of Peter, John, and Matthew so long ago and bid them to come, He offers to us the same summons:

Then he said to them all: "Whoever wants to be my disciple must deny themselves and take up their cross daily and follow me."
—Luke 9:23 NIV

If we choose to accept His life-changing invitation to follow Him, we must understand that this call comes with conditions. One of the prescribed conditions is to accept His cross and take up our own cross daily for the journey. Will you take it up? Will you deny yourself?

I have wondered at times if taking up one's cross is a singular cross or a once-in-a-lifetime event, but as I have traveled through the decades of life, I can assure you that I have had to *take up my cross* daily in a myriad of ways, both big and small. I have been given the opportunity to take up my cross each time I have been given the chance to die for the greater cause of Christ.

Whenever my will comes in opposition to the will of the Father, I am given the chance to die to self and to live for Christ alone. Because I am so very human on most days of my life, I have been given this extraordinary opportunity to *take up my cross* thousands upon thousands of times.

If I refuse to take up my cross as I follow Christ in discipleship, my heart will be littered with offenses, selfishness, and pride. I will trip over opinions, self-indulgence, and minor events. My life will never become the showplace of God's glory that it was designed to be without a continual and daily dying to self.

If you are married, that is the most meaningful arena in which you will be called to die to self. If you are not married, the Lord will give you opportunities in the single life to die to self on a daily basis. If you are a mother, you will die to self daily; if you are not a mother, your life will still offer wrenching opportunities to take up your cross and follow Christ.

When Jesus took up His cross, not only was He humbly accepting the pain that the cross entailed, but, more importantly, He was saying a resounding, "Yes!" to the will of the Father. As the disciples of Christ in the twenty-first century, we must be willing to say, "Yes!" to God in small ways, in painful ways, and in the large issues of life.

When a friend hurts us, we say, "Yes!" to forgiveness and to humility.

When cancer invades our lives, we say, "Yes!" to taking joy to doctors' offices, operating rooms, and to others who are suffering.

When a dream dies, we say, "Yes!" to partnering with God in dreaming a new dream and in setting a new goal.

When rejection hammers us, we say, "Yes!" to acceptance in the beloved of Christ.

Heart Inspection

What does it mean to be a disciple of Christ?

_____

_____

What does it mean to you, personally, to *take up your cross daily and follow Christ?*

_____

_____

How has Christ called you to die to self over the years?

_____

_____

Heartfelt Prayer

Jesus, I want to be Your disciple, therefore, I submit myself to Your way and to Your plan. I will carry my cross and follow You all the days of my life. I say, "Yes!" to the plans and purposes of God. In Jesus's name, I pray. Amen.

Eternal Words

Truly, truly I say to you, unless a grain of wheat falls into the earth and dies, it remains alone; but if it dies, it bears much fruit. —John 12:24

Cleaning Supplies

Read Philippians 3:1–14.

Part Eight:
The Dining Room –
Serve a Generous Portion of
Your Faith to Others

The gospel comes with a house key.
—Rosaria Butterfield

You were not saved for yourself, nor were you rescued from your sins just so that you could live a life of ease. You were saved to make an impact on the world around you. Jesus longs to overflow from your heart into the hearts of others. Whether you invite someone for coffee, pray for a woman at the grocery store, or go on a missions' trip, you are called to be a living, breathing demonstration of the gospel of Jesus Christ.

DAY 50

A Seat at Your Table

You have received a compelling assignment for your one extraordinary life. This assignment is not for the faint of heart, nor is it to be ignored. Although everyone receives much the same assignment in Christ, the individual call is still dominant. You are called to do what no one else can do. With your specific gifts, talents, personality, and sphere of influence, you are called to bring others to the table of Christ. What an honor is yours!

You are called to make hell smaller and heaven bigger! The voice of Reinhard Bonnke, the great theologian and missionary, resounds beyond the years of his life and calls each one of us: "Plunder hell in order to populate heaven!"

The reason that you are still alive today is to lead someone else to Christ. If you are wondering what God's will is for your life, it can be summed up in nine simple words: you are here to tell the story of Jesus.

You are here to encourage the discouraged, to pray for the sick, and to inject hope into hopeless hearts. You are here to sing a song of joy for the weary, to have a conversation with the lonely, and to smile at strangers. You are here to be the hands and feet of Jesus at this moment in history.

As God the Father looked across the canyons of time, He knew that there would be a lack of *"Godness"* in the twenty-first century. He saw aching souls, disheartened widows, grieving mothers, searching teenagers, and rejected women, and He knew that He must do something about it. But what could He do?

As He pondered what the answer to this lack might be, He thought of you! You are here to bring the nature and character of God to all that is evil, sick, and impure. You are here to demonstrate Jesus!

You are here to love difficult people, to forgive offenders, and to fight for the rights of the weak. You are here to welcome those who have no place to go.

Unfortunately, we live at a time in the culture of the world when people mistakenly believe that life is *"all about me."* We fictionally assume that the world revolves around our heart's desires; if conditions become too difficult or burdensome, we conjure up the falsehood that we must not be living in God's will for our lives.

The truth is that life has always been hard, and God has always been good. The truth is that we have always been God's answer to a world in abject pain. The truth is that we all wear an invitation that says, "Come to the table of the Lord."

Perhaps it's time for you to seriously consider the purpose of your life and daily commit to making room for someone else at the table of your heart.

This quote from Charles Spurgeon has always caused me to check my motives, my commitment, and my life calling. Perhaps it will do the same for you:

> If sinners be damned, at least let them leap to Hell over our bodies. If they perish, let them perish with our arms about their knees. Let no one go there unwarned and unprayed for.

Heart Inspection

Who first told you about Christ? Have you ever thanked that person?

_____

_____

How old were you when you received Christ as your Savior?

_____

_____

Have you ever led anyone to the Lord?

_____

_____

Heartfelt Prayer

Jesus, if You can use me in any way, I am available. I give all that I am to Your purposes and plans. In Jesus's name, I pray. Amen.

Eternal Words   _____

> *Behold, I stand at the door and knock; if anyone hears My voice and opens the door, I will come in to him and will dine with him, and he with Me.*   —Revelation 3:20

_____

The Main Course

Read Mark 16:14–20.

The Menu

I have a friend who calls himself a *foodie*; he enjoys the flavors, textures, and tastes of every morsel of food that he places into his often-open mouth. Generally, when we are deciding where to eat, if my foodie-friend is with us, he will inject his opinion with words such as:

+ "Let's not go there! The salads there are always wilted."
+ "I won't ever eat there again! Their portions are just too small."
+ "Nope! That's not an option for me! Not unless you all want heartburn from too much grease!"

We live in a world of *foodies*, my friend! The flavor of your life makes a difference to those in your sphere of influence. What are you serving with your life? A side dish of bitterness? An hors d'oeuvre of negativity? A constant diet of complaint?

When people enter into relationship with a follower of Christ, there should an abundance of joy with every meal.

Create in me a clean heart, God, and renew a steadfast spirit within me. Do not cast me away from Your presence, and do not take Your Holy Spirit from me. Restore to me the joy of Your salvation, and sustain me with a willing spirit. Then I will teach wrongdoers Your ways, and sinners will be converted to You. —Psalm 51:10–13

The psalmist was crying out to the Lord for a much-needed change in his life. He knew that he was desperately lacking a vital component in his heart, so he asked for joy. The development of these four verses is fascinating as we observe what this man of faith asked for:

Clean heart + steadfastness + Lord's presence + Holy Spirit + joy + willing spirit = Ministry

When the joy of the Lord has been restored to even a common sinner, a miracle happens! People will want what you have been given! When you exhibit a spirit of joy, as this psalm explains, wrongdoers will then listen to you. When you are a show and tell of the Lord's presence, where there is always fullness of joy, sinners will want what you have—more of Jesus!

So, what is on the menu of your heart? Perhaps it is time to add the word "joy" to the list of options that people will be able to choose from when they encounter your captivating life. The world is starving for joy—will you share it with them?

Heart Inspection

How can you use joy to lead someone to Christ?

_____

_____

How can you help others grow and find more joy in their faith?

_____

_____

Heartfelt Prayer

Jesus, I pray that You will restore to me the joy of Your salvation. I also pray that You will increase my ministry. Allow me the honor of leading sinners to Your throne room of grace! In Jesus's name, I pray. Amen.

Eternal Words

Do not grieve, for the joy of the Lord is your strength.
—Nehemiah 8:10 NIV

The Main Course

Read Psalm 16.

The Disciples Died for You

Peter, James, and John had all walked and talked with Christ. Matthew, Andrew, and Bartholomew were there when the loaves and fish were multiplied, when the raging storm was calmed, and when Lazarus was raised from the dead. Thomas, Philip, and the rest of the disciples gloriously saw Jesus risen from the dead and ascend into heaven!

They had known Jesus in the flesh and had believed that He was indeed the Messiah, both before and after His death and resurrection. After His ascension, these chosen men, each undoubtedly heaven-bound, could have chosen to live a quiet, inconsequential existence of contentment and comfort. They could have chosen to go back to their professions and to their families, knowing that heaven was in their future.

But they couldn't live that way; their faith was fierce and their calling was relentless. They lived to tell others what they had learned from Jesus. These young, largely uneducated men embraced the words of the Great Commission and refused to settle for the mediocre and mundane.

Jesus came up and spoke to them, saying, "All authority in heaven and on earth has been given to Me. Go, therefore, and make disciples of all the nations, baptizing them in the name of the Father and the Son and the Holy Spirit, teaching them to follow all that I commanded you; and behold, I am with you always, to the end of the age. —Matthew 28:18–20

Perhaps you might be interested in knowing how these men eventually died.

Peter was crucified on a cross upside down because he didn't feel worthy to be killed in the same manner as his Savior.

Andrew, Peter's brother, is believed to have been scourged and then tied rather than nailed to a cross so that he would suffer longer. According to a fifteenth century religious historian, Dorman Newman, Andrew lived for two days on that cross while preaching to those who were passing by.

John likely died of old age after preaching and writing of Christ his entire adult life.

James was killed by Herod with a sword; Bartholomew was reported to have been skinned alive and beheaded. Philip was either crucified or hung until he was dead; Thomas was stabbed with a spear in India.

Matthew was a missionary to Africa and was reported to have been impaled to the earth by spears and perhaps beheaded in the process.

I will spare you the details of the deaths of the other disciples, but I can assure you that they all died serving Christ and spreading the gospel. These young men, although their eternity was secured, chose to give their lives for the cause of Christ. They died so that you and I would know about Jesus.

Heart Inspection

Why is it difficult to tell others about Jesus?

_____

_____

Have you ever suffered for your faith?

_____

_____

What does the Great Commission mean to you personally?

_____

_____

Heartfelt Prayer

Jesus, give me courage when I am afraid and boldness to tell Your story so that others may learn of the salvation that only comes through You. I say, "Yes!" to the Great Commission of Christ. In Jesus's name, I pray. Amen.

Eternal Words

Therefore I urge you, brothers and sisters, by the mercies of God, to present your bodies as a living and holy sacrifice, acceptable to God, which is your spiritual service of worship. —Romans 12:1

The Main Course

Read Ephesians 4.

Preparing the Meal

I often invite guests to my home for a delightful luncheon, a delicious dinner, or a holiday celebration. In doing so, I have been known to spend several days in preparation for the much-anticipated event. First, I develop a menu, followed by a long and detailed grocery list. I polish silver and make sure that there are no dust bunnies to be found in my home. I determine what tablecloth I will use, what flowers I will display, and what the seating chart will be. It requires great concentration and diligent preparation to treat others with excellence and with care!

But in your hearts revere Christ as Lord. Always be prepared to give an answer to everyone who asks you to give the reason for the hope that you have. But do this with gentleness and respect.

—1 Peter 3:15 NIV

Just as preparing for an evening of conversation and food around a table requires diligent preparation, so does sharing one's faith. What does the preparation entail so that you are ready to give a reason for the hope that you have?

Remind yourself that everyone is hungry. Some people might be hungry for joy while others are starving for hope. Some folks are desperate for a healing while others are famished for a single drop of peace. Every person you meet today is hungry for something that you already have because you have Christ!

Remind yourself that God wants to use you! God has divine appointments for you today, so be very aware of who He brings into your life. God has a schedule planned just for you, so be wide awake and ready for a new person, a new friend, or a hurting soul.

Talk to yourself. Rehearse your hope and know what you might say to a lonely person, someone who is sick, or one who is filled with negativity. Practice giving your testimony to yourself so that you can press "play" when the need arises.

Read your Bible. Ask God to give you daily manna to share with someone else. If you never read your Bible, you might not be prepared when the need arises!

Pray to be surprised! We serve a God who loves to surprise His children. Don't you know that Peter was surprised to preach to thousands? Can you imagine the incredulity of Peter and John when they saw the lame man at the temple gate? Surprise is all in a day's work for the men and women of God at any moment in history.

Ask a question. People respond to interest; if you can ask someone a meaningful question, they are likely to answer it. I have a friend who, when placing her order in a restaurant, will say to the unsuspecting waitress, "My friends and I are about to pray over our food. Is there anything that we can pray for you about?"

How wonderful to be prepared to partner with the Father! Are you ready?!

Heart Inspection

What is your favorite Bible verse to share with others?

Has God ever surprised you with an opportunity or an appointment?

If you could lead anyone to the Lord, who would you want it to be?

Heartfelt Prayer

Jesus, show me how to prepare for service in Your kingdom. Give me divine appointments daily and surprise me with Your plans for my life! In Jesus's name, I pray. Amen.

Eternal Words

Preach the word; be ready in season and out of season; correct, rebuke, and exhort, with great patience and instruction.   —2 Timothy 4:2

The Main Course

Read Colossians 3:23–25 and Colossians 4:1–6.

All in a Day's Work

I am the mother of five extraordinary human beings who are separated in age by over thirteen years. When all five of my brood lived at home, from the very youngest to the oldest, they knew what to expect on a Saturday morning. There would be no watching cartoons, playing ball in the yard, or going to the park until their personal chore list was completed. On the seventh day of the week, as they came downstairs to scrounge around for pancakes, cereal, or last night's pizza, there were inevitably five lists on the kitchen table, each headlined with a name.

+ Matthew
+ Christopher
+ Jordan
+ Joy
+ Joni

Under each child's name were age-appropriate chores that were to be completed that very morning.

+ Fold the laundry
+ Clean the upstairs bathroom
+ Vacuum the family room
+ Clean out the car
+ Unload the dishwasher

As the mother of this creative, busy group of children, I knew that in order to function as a family at optimum capability, we would all need to pitch in. God, your Father, knows much the same thing about you.

For we are His workmanship, created in Christ Jesus for good works, which God prepared beforehand so that we would walk in them.
—Ephesians 2:10

God has a chore list with your name on it! He wants you to excel in all that is good and useful during your tenure on Earth. He longs for you to live exuberantly, fully, enthusiastically, and with divine purpose. You are

His masterpiece, and He wants to use you, His incredible creation, in His unshakable kingdom every day that you are sucking in oxygen.

Your chore list might look something like this:

+ Pray for someone today
+ Send money to a missionary
+ Write a book
+ Love a child
+ Invent something new
+ Discover a cure
+ Write a new song
+ Cook a meal for someone
+ Write a note to a lonely person
+ Give someone a hug
+ Smile at a stranger
+ Bake cookies for the neighborhood children
+ Love a difficult person
+ Tell somebody about Jesus!

You will discover, my friend, that when your life is in submission to the greater will of the Father, meaningful conversations and worthwhile appointments are all in a day's work.

Heart Inspection

What do you feel like your personal assignment is from God?

_____

_____

What does it mean to you that you are God's *workmanship* or *masterpiece*?

_____

_____

What assignment from the potential chore list will you accept as your own today?

_____

_____

Heartfelt Prayer

Jesus, use me. Remove my own self-imposed limitations and give me a list of what I can accomplish for You in Your kingdom! In Jesus's name, I pray. Amen.

Eternal Words

*And He made from one man every nation of mankind to live on all the face of the earth, having **determined** their appointed times and the boundaries of their habitation, that they would seek God, if perhaps they might feel around for Him and find Him, though He is not far from each one of us; for in Him we live and move and exist.*

—Acts 17:26–28

The Main Course

Read 1 Thessalonians 5.

A Table for One

One of the challenges you may face while serving in the kingdom of Christ is that it is often a lonely and unappreciated task. When no one else joins you in the simplest of assignments, will you fulfill your role even then? Although Jesus sent the disciples out two by two, sometimes we find in our modern world that the call to ministry involves a solitary commitment. Do you remember the lyrics to the simple song, "I Have Decided to Follow Jesus"? I have thought of this impactful line often through the years: "Though none go with me, I still will follow."

In *Prince Caspian*, written by the great scholar and theologian C. S. Lewis, Lucy was awakened from a sound sleep after hearing "the voice she liked best in the world" calling her name. She went off into the woods and found the great Lion, Aslan, "shining white in the moonlight." She had seen him before in this tale from *The Chronicles of Narnia*, but her siblings did not and blamed Lucy's imagination.

> "Now, child," said Aslan…"I will wait here. Go and wake the others and tell them to follow. If they will not, then you at least must follow me alone."
>
> It is a terrible thing to have to wake four people, all older than yourself and all very tired, for the purpose of telling them something they probably won't believe and making them do something they certainly won't like. "I mustn't think about it, I must just do it," thought Lucy.

Lucy obeyed Aslan, and her siblings eventually followed her. In this beloved allegory, when they finally saw Aslan, he looked "so majestic that they felt as glad as anyone can who feels afraid, and as afraid as anyone can who feels glad."

If God bids you to tell someone how to find Him, you must do it, even if you must do it alone. There are times when you must not think about it in a natural sense, but just do it because you have heard His voice. Fear and other atrocious emotions will always endeavor to convince you that your calling is unimportant and that there are others who will do a better job than you could ever do in fulfilling the plan of God. You must answer the voice of fear with the whisper of faith and say with Isaiah, *"Here am I. Send me!"* (Isaiah 6:8).

+ If God has called you to teach Sunday school, arise and go.
+ If the Lord has nudged you to teach a Bible study, arise and go.
+ If the Lord has asked you to send a teenager to camp, arise and go.
+ If the Lord has encouraged you to take a widow out to coffee, arise and go.

Just as a young girl obeyed Narnia's King and took the wonderful news to her siblings, so must you obey and tell others. Arise, my friend, and go. Go alone if you must, but go. There is a world waiting to hear the wonderful news of Jesus!

Heart Inspection

How do you know that you are called to service in the kingdom of God?

_____

_____

What risk is God asking you to take in order to serve Him with passion?

_____

_____

Heartfelt Prayer

Jesus, here I am. I stand here with all of my frailties, sin nature, and doubts, and yet I boldly come to You and say, "Here am I! Send me!" I am ready to do Your will. In Jesus's name, I pray. Amen.

Eternal Words

Then I heard the voice of the Lord, saying, "Whom shall I send, and who will go for Us?" Then I said, "Here am I. Send me!"

—Isaiah 6:8

Main Course

Read 1 Samuel 3.

DAY 56
Come and Dine

I'd like to tell you a story today, a paraphrased parable from the greatest Book ever written, told by the greatest Man who ever lived.

A rich, generous man decided to have a wonderful feast. After much preparation, when the day of the dinner arrived, the host told his servants to inform the invited guests that it was time. Everything was ready for their arrival and for their enjoyment!

One by one, however, these honored and much-anticipated guests began to make excuses as to why they were unable to attend the banquet given in their honor.

"I just bought some new property," explained one of the guests. "I must go look it over."

Another invited guest excused himself by saying, "I just purchased some new oxen and I have to make sure that they are able to plow my land."

A third guest said, "I am married. I need to spend time with my wife."

The disappointed servant came back and told his master what the guests had said. The master was rightfully angry at those who had declined his invitation. He then instructed his servant, "Go into the city and invite anyone you lay eyes on! Invite the poor, the blind, the disabled, the infirm, the hurting, and the lonely. Invite them to come! There is room at my table for them!"

After the servant had obeyed his master, he returned home and reported, "Sir, I have done what you asked me to do and there is still room at the table."

So the master replied, "Go out again. Go places you have not been before. Bring anyone you can find back with you to my banquet meal. Insist that they come and enjoy the meal that I have prepared for them!"

What a heart-stirring story! You may have recognized it from Luke 14:16–24 and realize that the master of the home represents the Lord while the servant represents you and me. We are the ones charged with bringing people into the house of the Lord to feast on His riches and His kindness. Some will make excuses while others will be honored to come.

The words of the master are most interesting to me as I ponder my calling in the kingdom of God. The master actually said to his servant, "*Go out to the roads and country lanes and **compel** them to come in, so that my house will be full*" (Luke 14:23 NIV).

The word for "compel" in biblical Greek is *anagkazo*. It is not a tender word nor is it a gentle word. *Anagkazo* means "to force," "to drive," or "to necessitate." As the servants of the Master, we are to be relentless in our pursuit of those under our watch. We should not give up, give in, or give out in our call to spread the gospel; instead, we are commanded to give every ounce of our energy in filling up the banquet room of God!

Eternity is at stake, and our assignment is clear: "Pummel hell and populate heaven!"

Heart Inspection

Today, I want you to make a list of five people whom you are committed to pray for and share the gospel with. Don't give up, my friend! Eternity is just one breath away.

1. _____
2. _____
3. _____
4. _____
5. _____

Heartfelt Prayer

Jesus, give me the boldness of Daniel and the resolve of Esther. Give me the persuasive abilities of Peter and the wisdom of Paul. Help me to invite people to Your banquet. In Jesus's name, I pray. Amen.

Eternal Words

> Just as you know how we were exhorting and encouraging and imploring each one of you as a father would his own children, so that you would walk in a manner worthy of the God who calls you into His own kingdom and glory. —1 Thessalonians 2:11–12

Main Course

Read Luke 14:15–24.

Part Nine: Knickknacks –
Daily Wisdom for Your Heart

Do little things as if they were great, because of the majesty of the
Lord Jesus Christ who dwells in thee.
—Blaise Pascal

There are issues in all of our hearts that are just a little bit here
and a little bit there. Although these issues don't fit *exactly* into
one specific room, they are a part of our lives and decorate various corners of our hearts. This week, in closing, we will be studying those nuances that are just "a little bit of this and a little bit of
that." Perhaps we could file these various items under the head-
ing of "wisdom," "creativity," or even "sweet trivia."

A Lamp

A home becomes a dark, dreary place without lamps of various shapes and sizes scattered around the rooms. Even a small lamp is able to shed light on dark corners, prevent injury, and warm a room with its cheery glow.

Your word is a lamp to my feet and a light to my path.
—Psalm 119:105

In ancient days, when this psalm was written, there were no traffic lights, street lamps, or flashlights. The patriarchs of our faith lived in an extremely dark world, and at nighttime, it was dangerous to walk anywhere without some type of light source.

The ingenuity of these early men and women gave them an answer to the lack of light they dealt with when the sun was long set and the moon was new. They decided to tie a small tin cup to a piece of leather and then attach it onto the toe piece of their sandals. When dusk began to fall, these resourceful folks then placed about a tablespoon of oil into the tin cup and lit it with a flame. This small foot lamp gave an adequate beam of light as they walked along the unlit pathways of their region.

Although the tiny lamp only shed about twelve or eighteen inches of light in front of their feet, it was just enough to keep the brave hikers from tripping over roots or rocks, from stepping on scorpions or other creatures, and keep them on their intended pathways.

The psalmist lovingly reminds us of the power of God's Word to light our pathways, whether we live in ancient times or in the electric days of the twenty-first century. In the modern world, we take light for granted, don't we? We flick on a switch and our entire home lights up immediately. We start our car and its headlights flood the way in front of us.

The courageous men and women of biblical times wanted just enough light for the next step. The psalmist reminds humanity from every generation that it is the Bible that will serve as a lamp to our feet and a light to our pathway. The Word of God is able to shed more light on a subject than modern technology ever will. Scripture gives enormous wisdom for all of life's conundrums and for every dark alley you encounter.

When you are dealing with doubt, read the Bible. When you are discouraged, spend some time in the Word. When your heart is troubled, open up the sacred pages of Scripture. It will give you all the light you could ever need.

Heart Inspection

When you are troubled in life, what is your first *go-to*?

_____

_____

Has the Bible ever brought faith to one of your doubts? Write about that here.

_____

_____

Have you memorized a Scripture verse this week yet? Why don't you choose one and begin to do so today.

_____

_____

Heartfelt Prayer

Lord Jesus, thank You for the light of the Bible. Thank You that Your Word will always give me just enough light for the next step. In Jesus's name, I pray. Amen.

Eternal Words

For the commandment is a lamp and the teaching is light; and rebukes for discipline are the way of life.　　　　　—Proverbs 6:23

Words of Wisdom

Read Psalm 119:97–128.

A Timepiece

Time! Where does it go? Tick, tock, tick, tock...

In the entryway of my childhood home, there stood a grandfather clock that had belonged to my paternal grandfather. Grandfather Burton had been a Cornell-educated lawyer and the clock was one of the treasures that my father inherited from his father. Throughout every day of my childhood, I could hear that massive clock tick away the seconds and the minutes. There was not a day of my growing up years, that Father Time did not seriously and perpetually "bong" away the hours of my life. I can still hear that immense timekeeper in my memory even today.

It seems like just yesterday that I was a little girl who loved to read and play the piano. Now I am a grandmother whose eyes are growing dim and whose joints no longer have young elasticity.

Time! Where does it go? Tick, tock, tick, tock...

If I find in myself desires which nothing in this world can satisfy, the only logical explanation is that I was made for another world.
—C. S. Lewis

I remind my grown children that although when they look at me, their mother, they see a woman over six decades old whose skin is a bit wrinkled and whose hair is graying, what they don't realize is that inside, I'm still the teenager who played the oboe...the college girl who was desperately homesick...the bride who was head over heels in love...and the young mom who loved rocking her babies. I am still all of those women!

Time! Where does it go? Trying to hold onto time is like trying to grasp the wind or save laughter in a bottle. The only answer to the conundrum of time is that we were not made for a limited measurement of time, but we were made for unlimited eternity.

You were placed here to train for eternity. Your body was only intended to be a house for your immortal spirit. It is flying in the face of God's purposes to do as many do—to make the soul a servant to the body, and not the body a servant to the soul.

—J. C. Ryle

Time gobbles up our days incessantly, but eternity extravagantly expands us. Time waits for no man, but eternity never ends. Time taps its foot at our expense while eternity welcomes us in its long embrace.

*But do not let this one fact escape your notice, beloved, that with the Lord one day is like a **thousand years**, and a **thousand years** like one day.*   —2 Peter 3:8

This Scripture has often troubled and confused me. I had never been able to discern its inspired meaning until one day I took the *time* to ask for guidance from the Holy Spirit. This is what I heard in the deepest place of my soul: "When you give just one day of your life to the Lord, He can give you one thousand years of impact in that small space of time. When you partner with the Lord on an ordinary day, He can give you the influence that others will require one thousand years to obtain."

We were made for eternity, not for years.

Heart Inspection

Do you consider time to be your enemy or your friend? Why?

What is your happiest memory?

What are you looking forward to in the years to come?

Heartfelt Prayer

Jesus, thank You for being Lord of time and eternity. I pray that You will give my life the impact of a thousand years! In Jesus name, I pray. Amen.

Eternal Words

> *For a thousand years in Your sight are like yesterday when it passes by, or like a watch in the night.* —Psalm 90:4

Words of Wisdom
Read Ecclesiastes 3.

A Masterpiece on the Refrigerator Door

Oh, to be a child again! Oh, to experience the marvel of caterpillars… clouds shaped like elephants…and the first strawberry of spring! Oh, to anticipate Christmas morning…the final day of school…and the first day of summer with childlike wonder!

A home with a child in residence is home to silly songs, missing puzzle pieces, and a creative masterpiece on the refrigerator door.

The years that belong only to childhood swiftly fly by and vanish, much the same as morning dew on grass. And yet, childhood lingers on in the deepest part of our heart like an obscure cottage hidden down a garden walkway.

There is an unseen child in each one of us who is waiting to rediscover the wonder of an ordinary day. Do you see that little girl knocking on the door of your heart? Perhaps she is there by God's design. Imagine that!

At that time the disciples came to Jesus and said, "Who then is greatest in the kingdom of heaven?" And He called a child to Himself and set him among them, and said, "Truly I say to you, unless you change and become like children, you will not enter the kingdom of heaven. So whoever will humble himself like this child, he is the greatest in the kingdom of heaven. And whoever receives one such child in My name, receives Me. —Matthew 18:1–5

Jesus bids us to discern, once again, all of the delights of living in the world of a child. This discovery will usher us into astonishment over what kingdom living was always meant to be. We will splash in joy and dress up in hope. We will toss around kindness like a sweet game to share with unsuspecting friends. We will share the treats of the fruit of the Spirit, and when the juice of those delicacies runs down our chins, we will giggle for more.

As children in the stunningly real kingdom of the Father, we will hang out of the windows of faith and believe for a brighter day. We will scamper up and down the hallways of righteousness, knowing that we will never get lost.

Finally, best of all, we will run into the arms of the One who can't wait to hold us and then hear our stories of valiant exploits or of our deepest desires in life. As children, we rest in His arms, on His lap, and we feel the unmatched security of unconditional love.

> Christ wants a child's heart, but a grown-up's head. He wants us to be simple, single-minded, affectionate, and teachable, as good children are; but He also wants every bit of intelligence we have to be alert at its job, and in first-class fighting trim.
>
> —C. S. Lewis

Heart Inspection

Have you become "too big for your britches"? How can you, in a practical way, embrace the joy of childhood once again?

_____

_____

What is your favorite childhood memory?

_____

_____

Who was your best friend in childhood?

_____

_____

Heartfelt Prayer

> Lord Jesus, give me a childlike heart so that I am able to rediscover the delight of living a life of faith and hope in Your unshakable kingdom. In Jesus's name, I pray. Amen.

Eternal Words

> _They who seek the_ Lord _will not lack any good thing. Come, you children, listen to me; I will teach you the fear of the_ Lord.
>
> —Psalm 34:10–11

Words of Wisdom

Read 1 Samuel 1.

A Fire in the Fireplace

For most of human history, family life was dictated by the strength of the fire in the center of the home. This fire was used to boil water for cleanliness, to keep the family warm in winter, to shed light throughout the home, and to cook the daily meals that nourished their bodies. The family did not dare to let the fire go out or weaken, even during the summer months, because their lives would be severely impacted by the absence of the fire.

Do you have a fire burning in the center of your heart? Is there a hot, bright place inside of you that disappointment does not have the power to extinguish and people's words cannot dampen?

It is the fire of passion that I am referring to—a hot spot of sustenance, holiness, and hope.

You have been created *on* purpose, *with* purpose, and *for* purpose. You are God's strategic and vital idea for this moment in history. Are you partnering with God in keeping the flame of devotion burning brightly? Do you have a purposeful passion that guides the days of your life and provides nourishing sustenance for your soul?

Your passion should be your first thought in the morning and your last thought at night as you lay your head upon your pillow. Your passion consumes your future plans and dictates your priorities.

> The secret of the Christian's passion is simple: Everything we do in life we do it as to the Lord and not to men. —David Jeremiah

A wonderful aspect of abundant living is discovering purpose and then fanning the flame of this invigorating aspiration. Perhaps your calling is to teach children, lead short-term missions' trips, or run for public office. Maybe the flame of your passion is kindled by leading others in worship, serving in the medical field, or praying for others. This overriding fire of purpose is where your interests and talents collide with a world in pain. This holy collision causes the fire to burn even more intensely; however, this sacred fire is not one of decimation, but it is a fire of God's very presence.

There is a fire of God's specific intention for your life that is meant to burn brightly within your heart all the days of your life. Don't let the fire of purpose diminish! This flame of divine origination will feed you, warm you, brighten your life, and keep you close to the cleansing power of Christ Himself.

> A great leader's courage to fulfill his vision comes from passion, not position. —John C. Maxwell

Heart Inspection

What is the fire that burns brightly within your heart? Can you give a name to it?

_____

_____

What is the greatest need that you see in the world today? How can you help to meet this need?

_____

_____

What do you love most about serving Christ?

_____

_____

Heartfelt Prayer

> Jesus, let me burn brightly for You! Light the flame of holy desire in my heart and let this fire lead me and guide me all the days of my life. In Jesus's name, I pray. Amen.

Eternal Words

> *As for me, I baptize you with water for repentance, but He who is coming after me is mightier than I, and I am not fit to remove His sandals; He will baptize you with the Holy Spirit and fire.*
> —Matthew 3:11

Words of Wisdom
Read Acts 2:1–7.

Afterword: The Heart You Call Home

My prayer, as you gently close the pages of this devotional, is that your heart will be miraculously changed and strengthened forever.

I pray that the wisdom you acquired, the comfort you experienced, and the hope that was shared will fill every corner of your captivating heart for years to come.

I pray that as you gaze over the landscape of your past, you will count your blessings and bravely look to the future with anticipation and purpose.

I pray that you will know Him in His fullness—the One who made you, forgave you, and loves you for time and eternity.

I pray that your heart will overflow with the good theme of Christ and you will share your faith with the world around you.

I pray that your foundation will be solid and strong.

I pray that before you make another decision, you will read your Bible.

I pray that you will know the love of God that surpasses knowledge.

I pray that you will be devoted to prayer and know that you possess the power to change human history when you pray.

I pray that you will forever keep a song of worship in your heart.

I pray that when people experience relationship with you, they will be nourished by the fruits of the Holy Spirit in your life.

I pray that you will forgive easily and often, keeping the clutter of bitterness out of your glorious heart.

I pray that you will share your faith freely and extravagantly.

I pray that heaven will increase and that hell will decrease simply because you are alive.

And as you journey through life, I pray that the heart that you call home will be filled with rare and rich treasures that will point others to Jesus.

About the Author

The president and CEO of Carol McLeod Ministries, Carol McLeod is a popular speaker at women's conferences and retreats.

She is the author of a dozen books, including *Rooms of a Mother's Heart: A Sacred Call and an Eternal Purpose*; *Vibrant: Developing a Deep and Abiding Joy for All Seasons*; *Significant: Becoming a Woman of Unique Purpose, True Identity, and Irrepressible Hope*; *StormProof: Weathering Life's Tough Times*; *Guide Your Mind, Guard Your Heart, Grace Your Tongue*; *Joy for All Seasons*; *Holy Estrogen*; and *Defiant Joy*.

Carol hosts a twice weekly podcast, *A Jolt of Joy!* on the Charisma Podcast Network, and a weekly podcast, *Significant*. Her weekly blog, *Joy for the Journey*, has been named in the Top 50 Faith Blogs for Women. Carol also writes a weekly column in *Ministry Today*.

She has written several devotionals for YouVersion, including "21 Days to Beat Depression," which has touched the lives of nearly one million people around the world. Her teaching DVD *The Rooms of a Woman's Heart* won the prestigious Telly Award for excellence in religious programming.

Carol was the first women's chaplain at Oral Roberts University and served as chaplain on the university's Alumni Board of Directors for many years.

She has been married to her college sweetheart, Craig, for more than forty years and is the mother of five children in heaven and five children on earth. Carol and Craig also happily answer to "Marmee and Pa" for their captivating grandchildren.